Developing New Business Ideas
for AS Level

Polly Glegg, Nancy Wall and Jon Brook

Edited by: **Nancy Wall**

Polly Glegg teaches at Lea Valley High School in Enfield. She has 10 years' experience of teaching in inner London. She has a Master of Teaching degree from the Institute of Education in London, and has worked as an associate tutor on the MTeach programme. She is very active in the development of innovative teaching and learning resources, some of which can be found on the Edexcel Business and Economics website; these have proved to be very popular with teachers of both GCSE and A level courses. She contributes to 'Teaching Business and Economics', the magazine of the Economics, Business and Enterprise Association (EBEA).

Nancy Wall was a teacher for the first half of her career. Since 1991 she has worked in curriculum development, with a particular interest in teaching strategies and classroom resource development. She is currently reviews editor of 'Teaching Business and Economics', the magazine of the Economics, Business and Enterprise Association. She has long experience of writing and editing resources for students.

Jon Brook is Head of Business and Economics at Droitwich Spa High School and is experienced as an examiner and as a writer of classroom resources. He teaches everything from A Level Economics to BTEC First Enterprise and Entrepreneurship. He thinks that skills, rather than content, are what the students should really be learning when they come to school.

© Anforme Ltd 2012
ISBN 978-1-905504-72-5
Images supplied by Shutterstock.com

Anforme Ltd, Stocksfield Hall, Stocksfield, Northumberland NE43 7TN.

Typeset by George Wishart & Associates, Whitley Bay.
Printed by Potts Print (UK) Ltd.

Acknowledgements

The businesses that provided case studies for this book gave much help to the authors. Their contribution to the book has made a great difference. All of the case studies are either drawn directly from the real world or based on real-life situations encountered by the authors. We are particularly indebted to Abundant for their contributions, which involved lengthy interviews.

We are also indebted to Jenny Wales and Stephen Barnes; some of their past work that is now out of print has been included in certain chapters. We thank the Nuffield Foundation for permission to include this material.

Every effort has been made to trace the owners of copyright material, but in a very few cases this has proved to be impossible. We offer our apologies to any copyright holder whose rights may have been unwittingly infringed.

Contents

Introduction

Welcome to your companion book for unit 1 of Edexcel AS Business Studies and AS Economics and Business. You have chosen a book which is tightly mapped to the unit specification, containing examples and practical activities as well as practice exam-style questions. Working through all sections of the text should give you a clear understanding of the content needed to achieve well in your exam for this unit.

Developing New Business Ideas is all about how new business ideas are put into practice. This means that while reading this book you will learn a lot about entrepreneurs (people who set up their own businesses). You will also read some examples drawn from larger businesses because business theory can be applied equally well to large businesses as to small. If you are really serious about your studies in this subject, you must supplement the examples you find here with wider, up to date knowledge of the business environment. One of the most exciting aspects of your chosen subject is that is it all around you – you should relate all that you learn about theory to what you know of the contemporary environment. Discuss it with your friends and teachers; annotate class notes with your own ideas; and, above all, enjoy the process of developing your understanding of how business ideas are brought to market.

Suggested ways to use this book

Your teacher might choose to use this book with you in class, in which case follow her or his lead. If you are using it independently, you may like to:

- Read the opening case study and spend 5 or 10 minutes jotting down responses to the discussion topics. It is even better if you can actually discuss these with a friend.

- Read through the text of the chapter, including any worked examples.

- Update your glossary (which you should be keeping) with new vocabulary from the chapter.

- Carry out any suggested independent research activities such as exploring recommended internet sites.

- Make notes on the chapter – you could try summarising what you have learned
  - In a mind-map, *or*
  - In a diagram, *or*
  - On one side of A4 paper, *or*
  - In 100 words or less, then 50 words, then 25 words… what is the essence of the chapter?

- Write detailed answers to the exam-style questions at the end of the chapter.

The margins of the book are deliberately wide so that you have space to annotate the text. So long as you own the book (not if you have to give it back to your school, for example), you should use it like class notes and highlight, define, explain and illustrate parts of the text where this aids your understanding.

You may choose to hole-punch the book and file it with your class notes. This way you will always have it to hand and can easily cross-reference the contents of each chapter with other items in your notes.

You might notice that in a few places topics are not quite in the order of your specification. The purpose of this is to make the content a little easier to understand. If you have any difficulty finding a topic, use the index at the back of the book to help you.

Answering the exam-style questions

As you progress through your course you will do lots of work with your teachers on how to approach exam questions. Here are just a couple of general tips to help you out:

1. When you read a question, look for three things:

   (a) The **command word**. This tells you to 'describe', 'analyse', 'assess' etc. It is important because it lets you know which skills and assessment objectives are being assessed in your answer. Make sure you know what each command word is asking for.

   (b) The **number of marks** given. This gives you information about how to answer the question because you can see whether marks are given for each skill demonstrated (with low-mark answers) or for the level of response (higher mark answers). Understanding how to gain marks means that you can self-check your answers to see whether you have given the examiner what they need in order to award you full marks.

   (c) The **relevant theory**. Each question is testing your understanding of a piece of theory from the unit specification. You may have to apply this to a specific context, but before this you need to be clear on what the theory is. In this book the questions all relate to the chapter they are in, so this is pretty easy, but get in the habit now of thinking about the key pieces of theory before you start to write your answers.

2. **Application** is the skill of writing in context. To help you develop this skill when you read business case studies, as part of your wider reading and in sections B and C of the unit 1 exam paper, make brief notes using the acronym LOSER. Then draw on these notes when applying theory to the business:

   LO stands for long-term and short-term objectives

   What are the business's goals, overall and within the situation described in the case study? Any issues you highlight or suggested actions you identify should be relevant to the objectives of the business.

   S stands for stakeholders

   What groups of individuals have an interest in this business? Be as specific as you can, using the names of owners, for example, or listing the different suppliers if these are mentioned in the case study.

   E stands for environment

   Used here, this E refers to everything to do with the environment in which the business operates. Consider (briefly) the following:
   - *The market in which the business competes*
   - *Major competitors*
   - *Trends in the market*
   - *Economic conditions*
   - *Any other relevant SLEPT factors. SLEPT stands for: Social, Legal, Economic, Political, Technological. It is an acronym commonly used to embrace all aspects of the business environment.*

   R stands for resources.

   The E above asks you to look at factors which are beyond the business's control – these apply to all firms in the market. Resources are factors which are specific to the business and are not available to all firms... the opposite. Using resources effectively can give a firm a source of competitive advantage. This means a way to gain customers over competitors. Resources could include:
   - *Special staff skills and expertise*
   - *Money in the bank*
   - *A good reputation*
   - *Strong brands*
   - *A secure customer base*
   - *Access to particularly high quality raw materials, or to low cost materials.*

Effective independent study

Again, listen to your teacher for specific advice, but plan to include all of the following in your regular independent study timetable. Start early, work methodically, and by the time you sit your exam you will be ready to demonstrate effectively all that you have learned:

1. Read through class notes. Identify any areas which you feel less sure of and do some extra research on these. Annotate your class notes with what you have learned.

2. Update your glossary of key terms. Learning 'business' is like learning a language – you need to understand the meaning of many new words, and to use them effectively in your verbal and written communication. Practise using new words frequently.

3. Find relevant news and journal articles and add these to your file. Ideally, annotate each article to highlight key learning points and links to different parts of the unit specification.

4. Complete practice exam questions. Ask your teacher for a copy of the relevant mark scheme and, once you've answered the question, try to mark your own answer. Then annotate your work to show how you could improve the answer and gain full marks.

5. Watch, read or listen to a quality news source regularly (the BBC, or a broadsheet newspaper such as *The Times*, *The Independent* or *The Guardian*, for example). Consider how current affairs reflect some of the topics that you are learning about.

6. Talk to your peers about what you are learning. Regular study groups are one of the best ways to improve your revision since you can support each other, and by sharing your ideas you will embed and develop them.

OK, you're ready to begin. Work hard, enjoy your studies, and good luck.

Chapter 1

Characteristics of entrepreneurs

Abundant

Shane Wall has a history of making things happen: at 15 years old he was running discos in his local village; by the time he was 20 he had bought his own DJ equipment and had a successful business providing the entertainment at weddings, which he ran at the same time as working in a day job. Eventually Shane lost interest in this business and moved to London where he volunteered to gain work experience before eventually finding a job working for BBC Radio in technical administration. Shane moved jobs twice after this, ending up at a creative communications agency called Unique. (Much of Unique's business involved sound recording for the BBC and various radio stations.) Shane continued to run disco parties as a side-business in his free time.

In 1997 Shane set up a business with a friend running snowboarding holidays for groups of young party-goers. Shane's friend already had a clubbing business called Abundant Clubbing so they called this business Abundant Holidays. They used their access to clubbers who already knew the Abundant brand to target individuals with the money to spend on snowboarding – a fashionable new sport at the time which was gaining popularity. They would book the holidays, take over whole venues in the ski resort and fly in bands or DJs to run events in the evenings. By 1999 the friend had left the business and Shane had taken over ownership of Abundant Ltd.

Shane no longer runs holidays. In 2007 he was made redundant by Unique. Needing direction, Shane spent some time thinking about what he could do with his skills in technical administration and his experience of working at the communications agency. Unique had, by this time, given Shane experience in a diverse range of roles. So when a business contact called and asked him to do some freelance work for him, Shane spotted the opportunity to set up his own communications agency, producing adverts for radio stations, social media advertising and some radio programmes. He funded this with retained profit from the holiday business as well as personal savings.

Profit

Abundant is now a creative communications agency with Shane leading operations. He has brought in a Creative Director, James, who has added creative skills to Shane's technical expertise. A team of 10 staff members now work with Shane. He still works 14/15 hour days when necessary, sometimes 7 days a week. The business is busy, successful and growing.

Discussion points

(a) What personal qualities did Shane have that helped his business ideas to become a success?

(b) Why were these qualities necessary for Shane?

Entrepreneurial qualities

Entrepreneurs are people who have a business idea and make it happen. They set up and run their own businesses. They might be able to take on staff once the business is generating income but initially it is common for an entrepreneur to work alone or with a business partner to do all of the different tasks needed to make the idea happen. In fact, three quarters of all businesses in the UK have no employees so it is very common for entrepreneurs to carry out all of the work for their business alone.

It is not necessary to have studied Business to be an entrepreneur, nor do you have to have any business experience. However, there are some personal qualities or characteristics that make it more likely that a person will have a successful idea and be able see it through to completion.

A **characteristic** is a personal quality which an entrepreneur possesses.

An **entrepreneur** is a person who has ideas and makes them happen.

Profit is the financial reward to the owner of a business. It is the difference between **revenue** (money earned by the business) and **costs** (money spent by the business).

Entrepreneurial characteristics

Initiative

Initiative describes the quality of taking action without needing somebody else to tell you to do so or to give you direction. An entrepreneur who shows initiative won't simply sit and think about their idea – they will take action to make it happen.

For example, in the case study above the young Shane didn't just *think* that a disco would be good for the village – he went out and researched the cost of hiring equipment, and then he actually organised an event. Years later, when his friend offered him freelance work, the older Shane took the initiative in setting up his own agency, rather than continuing to work for another business.

Hard-working

Entrepreneurs often have their ideas while they are working in a job or raising a family or studying, so they have to carry out their research, plan how to launch their idea and then start to run their new business as well as meeting other commitments. Even when their business is running and they are working on it full time, entrepreneurs often work from early in the morning until late at night, including at weekends, to complete all the work that is needed.

You can see in the case study above that Shane worked on his disco, party and snowboarding businesses at the same time as working. He gave up lots of his spare time to launch his businesses and to make sure that he kept working to improve them. He now works long hours at Abundant when this is necessary, even if this means working during evenings and weekends.

What is the message?

Initiative

Hard work

Resilience

Being resilient

Resilience is the ability to withstand or recover from difficult situations. Entrepreneurs may face a range of difficult situations such as:

- periods of time when demand is low
- difficulties raising finance for **capital investment**
- customers making complaints or switching to competitors
- periods of high workload
- learning new business management skills or navigating unfamiliar laws or **regulations**
- times when things do not go according to plan.

Any of these situations could cause the entrepreneur to worry, struggle and perhaps eventually want to give up. The quality of resilience allows the entrepreneur to resist these feelings and to carry on until the difficult time has passed. Even when Shane was made redundant he didn't give up. Instead, he drew on the skills and experience that he had to make a new idea work.

Creativity

Being creative

Being creative means having original ideas. Persuading customers to give you their money can be a challenge – you have to convince them that the service or product that you are offering is worth spending their money on. The product must compare well with the alternative ways in which they might spend it. Entrepreneurs can use creativity in two ways:

- Designing a product or service that is unique in some way, so that customers believe that it is better than competitors' products or services. For example, Abundant Holidays offered a unique holiday experience by combining snowboarding holidays with parties and discos.

- In running the business. For example, an entrepreneur may think of new ways to advertise the product which will capture customers' interest. This is especially important for entrepreneurs who often lack the **working capital** necessary for traditional advertising in print media or on local radio. New media are opening up many opportunities for entrepreneurs to research and promote their ideas using, for example, blogs, pay-per-click advertising and social networking sites.

> **Regulations** are rules that businesses have to follow. These can be laws made by Parliament (for example, employment law) or rules written by an organisation which regulates a particular industry (such as the Advertising Standards Agency).
>
> **Capital investment** is spending on equipment and premises.
>
> **Working capital** is the money available to fund the day to day running of the business. (You will learn more about this on page 81.)

Find out

Explore www.abundant.co.uk to see how Shane is using creativity to promote his business as well as to differentiate the service that Abundant now provides.

Self-confidence

Being self-confident

Having self-confidence means believing in yourself. Setting up in business is inherently risky because it involves committing time and money to an idea that might not be successful. A BBC report in 2010 said that only 1 in 5 of all new business ideas will succeed, so entrepreneurs need to believe in their ideas and their ability to make them work.

Think

Which parts of Figure 3.1 do you think each of the leaders, in the opening case study of this chapter, might use? Explain your view.

Motivation means using the right strategy to help employees work more effectively. By meeting the needs of the business situation and the employees, leaders can increase commitment and so encourage hard work.

How do leaders perform their role?

There have been many attempts to identify the vital qualities of a good leader. There are three basic categories that can help to define leadership styles.

Leadership styles

● **Autocratic leaders** impose their decisions on the group. Commands are tightly specified with little or no allowance for discussion or individual choice. There may be little delegation of specific responsibilities. Rewards are unpredictable, and the leader's plans may remain obscure. Socially they will tend to keep their distance from their employees. Their primary concern will be the level of profit that can be achieved. Autocratic leadership is sometimes described as authoritarian.

● **Democratic leaders** encourage the group to participate in discussion and to feel that they have contributed to any final decision. The leader mixes informally with the group and is usually well-known at the personal level. Methods of work are left to individual choice, while rewards are open and fair in their distribution.

● **Paternalistic leaders** take into account the needs of all interest groups, be they customers, employees or shareholders, when making decisions. They will consult employees early on and explain the reasons for their subsequent decisions. They will look for ways to develop employees' skills and capabilities through regular training. They show concern for employees' wellbeing and social needs. Nevertheless, when it comes to the final decision, they will take it on their own.

Autocratic leaders take top-down decisions without consulting employees to find out their views. They may provide very little information on the reasons for the decision.

Democratic leaders guide rather than dictate, consulting widely and encouraging everyone to participate in the decision-making process.

Paternalistic leaders behave rather as a parent might in making family decisions. They consult at every level and explain their reasons, but take the final decision themselves.

Leadership decisions

In thinking about management and leadership styles, it is a good idea to remember what you learnt about characteristics of entrepreneurs. In many small businesses, some decisions may be decidedly risky. The entrepreneur may be facing a make or break choice, as a result of which the business may not survive. The group of employees being consulted may have ideas that can threaten the future of the company. You can see at once that leaders may need to adopt more than one leadership style if they are to make the most of the opportunities they have.

Show your understanding

Go back to leaders A, B and C in the opening case study. How would you classify them? Remember that leaders can exhibit more than one style of leadership. Explain your conclusions.

Do businesses X, Y and Z need specific leadership styles? Explain why they might (or might not).

Theory X and Theory Y

Douglas McGregor, a professor of management who worked at top US universities, wrote about these two theories of management in the 1950s. He believed that many managers make one of two assumptions about their employees.

McGregor

- **Theory X managers** take a rather cynical view, assuming that their employees will have little enthusiasm for work and will try to avoid making any great effort. Most will have little ambition and prefer not to take on responsibilities. Typically they will therefore need to be closely supervised, with strict rules and regulations and incentives to make them work effectively for the organisation.

- **Theory Y managers** see their employees quite differently; they assume that they will enjoy their work and will strive to contribute to the success of the organisation. They will respond when given responsibility and will use their ingenuity to solve problems if given a chance to do so.

Theory X and Theory Y can in certain circumstances be related to leadership styles, but often it is not so simple. McGregor thought that effective managers would be the ones who valued and trusted their employees; he saw lack of trust as leading to poor management. On the whole, recent trends in the workplace – towards an emphasis on teamwork and collaboration – have tended to support this view. But much depends on the specific requirements of the workplace in question. The management style used in, say, McDonalds might be very different from that in a business that looked to its employees to be creative. Google has made use of very distinctive strategies, for example by providing recreational areas for employees and expecting them to take breaks from their creative thinking to relax or play games. This might be completely inappropriate for a business relying on large numbers of part-time employees to deal quickly with customer requirements.

Theory X managers assume that their employees are lazy and prefer to be given firm direction with strict controls. Managers will adopt a stick and carrot approach to make them work hard. This may involve targets with heavy penalties if they are not met.

Theory Y managers assume that human beings want to work and will commit themselves to work effectively without strict controls. They will engage with the objectives of the organisation, accept responsibility and use their initiative to help solve problems.

Theory X vs Theory Y

Show your understanding

1. Write down three ways in which you might motivate a Theory X employee. (Theory X employees don't like things to change, are motivated by money, tend to dislike working, must be closely watched, and need to be told what to do because they are unlikely to make good decisions.)

2. Write down three ways you might motivate a Theory Y employee. (Theory Y employees enjoy their work, work hard to gain rewards, work independently, can be trusted to make good decisions and work unsupervised and are trustworthy and reliable.)

3. Explain three significant differences between the two approaches.

The following case studies concern very different businesses and provide examples of a range of leadership styles and management strategies.

Leaders

General Electric

Jack Welch went to work at General Electric, the giant US manufacturer when he was aged 21 in 1960. A very ambitious chemical engineer, he worked his way up the company ladder. By 1981 was company chairman and CEO. GE's annual sales revenue then was US$26 billion. In 2001 when he left, it was $130 billion. Yes, there was some inflation in that time but not enough to account for even half that growth.

Jack Welch managed GE partly by sheer force of personality and partly by meeting and remembering a huge number of his employees. He believed a large company should be run just like a small one that simply had to keep on growing. He gave his managers scope to think through the best ways for their divisions to expand. He gave them incentives too. But he had no hesitation in firing them if they were making losses when he thought they should make a profit.

He was prepared to delegate responsibility, yet he involved himself in everything that was happening. He listened carefully to his managers' ideas. If they did well, he gave them more freedom to decide how to expand. He backed them up so long as their ideas were working. He thought this approach helped to solve problems faster. All GE employees, whatever their level called him Jack. He used meetings purposefully to ensure that everyone felt involved, just as they would in a small company where everyone knew everyone else.

More than half Jack Welch's time was spent on people management. However, he was never an easy boss to work for. He wasn't concerned with making people happy. His message was 'succeed or you're fired'. Some people were critical of his methods. The pressure on employees was intense and may have led them to cut corners. He believed managers should earn high pay and was unconcerned about the difference between the highest and lowest levels of pay in the company.

Richer Sounds

Julian Richer opened his first Richer Sounds hi-fi store in 1978, aged just 19. He now has 50 outlets in the UK. He sees himself as a leader who empowers his staff. The company has a number of committees and colleagues are encouraged to join them. Some groups concentrate on aspects of cost control. Managers are expected to review the performance of other stores, and may be appointed as associate directors. They may be responsible for monitoring human resources (i.e. employees) and merchandising (promoting sales) in the stores. They are expected to listen carefully to what their staff say.

Everyone is encouraged to take on new responsibilities and to try new jobs. The company has a 'no failure' culture. There is no stigma attached to demotion. If someone finds they are not suited to a particular job or do not enjoy it, they can try something else.

The basic salary of employees is relatively low and is made up by performance-related incentive payments, suggestion payments and profit-sharing payments. These are designed to give employees a sense of ownership and to recognise and reward achievement. But recognition is not solely pay-related. Communication, praise and the creation of a climate where employees are valued, are all just as important to the Richer Sounds management style.

Leadership at Abundant

Remember Abundant, the creative agency in Chapter 1? Ed has worked at Abundant for 10 months. His job involves some creative work and some project management – seeing the work through to completion.

Each assignment starts with a pitch. Abundant will be asked how it would promote a film. The team will talk their ideas over and figure out what will attract customers. Creative ideas must be developed with very tight deadlines. Shane will cost the inputs and produce a quotation, with competitors' prices very much on his mind. If the pitch is successful, the work is delegated according to who has the skills to deal with each stage of production.

Ed will liaise with the client and the publishers, plan the media, schedule each stage and brief the designers. Often he will deal directly with customers. Shane is quick to get involved if anyone is not meeting deadlines. Ed says that if he gives an incomplete brief to the designers, they will not be able to do their job properly and within the team, there will be lots of pressure on him to do a better job. James, the creative director will always be keeping an eye on things.

The leadership function at Abundant is all about controlling creativity within a framework of tasks. The staff can discuss ideas all day but the job must be done on time. If it is not, the business is liable to lose its reputation, and probably the customer too. In common with many b2b organisations, (businesses that sell to other businesses), Abundant has a relatively small number of big customers, like the film companies. The loss of one customer could be a very serious matter. Abundant works like a factory – the job must be done. Ed stays behind, sometimes until 9pm, to get projects finished on time.

The creative team hard at work.

Show your understanding

1. Compare the leadership styles at GE, Richer Sounds and Abundant. Say which basic categories each might fall into and explain why. For each business, show what the leadership style may have contributed to the success of the business (so far).

2. To what extent do the three leaders of these businesses demonstrate Theory X or Theory Y assumptions?

3. What pressures do the employees face in each business?

4. Each of these businesses has had to face threats that could be serious, not least from recession. Think about what changes in leadership style might be significant in ensuring the survival of the business and explain your conclusions.

Do it

GE and Richer Sounds are respectively, a big international business and a medium sized business. Abundant is very small. Think about other small businesses you have come across. Do their owners have ways of managing that you can recognise in terms of the three leadership styles you have studied?

Interview the owner of a local business. Ask what leadership style they use, and find out why. (You may have to explain leadership styles to them.)

How do markets work?

Market stall

e-commerce

Supermarket

Estate agent

Discussion points

(a) What do all these markets have in common?

(b) What kinds of competition will each business face?

(c) What will happen to the estate agent if many people are experiencing rising incomes and want to buy bigger houses?

(d) In all these situations, the sellers are to some degree specialising. Why would they choose to do this?

Exchange

The key feature of a **market** is that there will be buyers and sellers. They will communicate, but not necessarily face-to-face. A deal takes place when both buyer and seller are ready to **exchange** something at a price they can agree on. Both of them will expect to be better off as a result of this deal. All they need is a satisfactory way of communicating with each other.

Specialisation

We need markets because we can't produce everything we need for ourselves. In prehistoric times many communities could produce most of what they needed. That still happens in very isolated places like the Amazon basin where there are still a few undisturbed tribes living traditional stone age-style lives. But the norm is for each of us to specialise in whatever we do best, and use the money we earn to buy what we need. **Specialisation** allows us to produce more and exchange makes it possible for us to get what we want. In primitive societies this would mean bartering – a direct swap of, say, food for clothing. In modern societies we use money to make it easy to buy a wide range of products.

> **Markets** exist wherever there are buyers and sellers who can communicate with each other and agree to buy or sell at a price that makes the transaction worthwhile.
>
> **Exchange** means selling what we have or can produce and using the money to buy what we want for ourselves.
>
> **Specialisation** means concentrating on creating the products we can make and sell most efficiently.

World markets

Generally, a market is not located in one specific place. It can be anywhere – in a shopping centre or on-line. But when we speak of markets, we are usually referring to the market as a whole – the housing market, the labour market or the market for cars. Often we will think about a national market but world markets are important too. The price of petrol often changes in response to conditions in the world market for crude oil.

Competition

Usually the seller sets the price but quite often prices change in response to circumstances. A market trader who is selling mushrooms at a higher price than other nearby stalls will not sell many, unless they are visibly fresher and better in quality. So the price will be affected by **competition** in the market. Sometimes people will haggle before agreeing on a price. The more sellers there are, the fiercer the competition will be.

The impact of competition

If you were the only person selling oranges in a street market, you could put the price up and still find quite a number of buyers. But the fact is that there will be many stalls selling oranges and they will compete for buyers by keeping their prices low. Consumers benefit. However, sellers will always try to avoid selling oranges – or anything else – at less than the price they paid for them.

Competition will not only affect prices. It also keeps businesses nimble, encouraging them in various ways to adapt to changing markets. They may:
- Try hard to develop new or innovative products – like the iPad
- Improve the design of existing products
- Look for new technologies or better management strategies that will help to cut costs, e.g. modernising their equipment or using labour saving devices.

Competition – the process by which businesses strive against one another to attract more customers by keeping prices down and making the product more appealing. The more sellers there are in the market the stiffer the competition will be, and the more likely it is that prices are as low as possible.

Smartphones and retailing

Gap found itself struggling recently with sluggish sales and some tired branding strategies. Now it is reaching out to its smartphone-carrying customers by making videos and promoting them through web links in its stores. One such video tells them about how to clean jeans by putting them in the freezer (properly wrapped up of course) where the cold will kill off any germs and bacteria.

Customers are still visiting High Street stores to look at and choose the clothes they like, but increasingly they are using their smartphones to find out about competing products and prices and then buying from on-line retailers. Gap believe they can fight back, engaging with customers by creating in-store experiences that their rivals may not have thought of.

Identify three products (or businesses) that typically compete on price and three that compete in other ways.

Different markets

Show your understanding
There are markets for products that are bought and sold and also for people who offer their services in the labour market. For each of the following, think about how much competition the product or the person might face, and why.
- Orange juice
- Fighter planes
- Computer programmers

eBay and the Stock Exchange are examples of markets. For each one, think about who the buyers and sellers are. Is there likely to be much competition in these markets? What might influence prices?

The prospect of profit provides an incentive to set up or expand a business.

Covering costs

Avoiding losses

In any market, no one will be willing for long to sell something for less than it costs to produce or to buy from suppliers. Now and then a business will sell a 'loss leader' at less than cost price. A retailer might price a popular product below cost, and advertise the fact, just to get a few new customers to come through the door and look around. But that kind of promotion will not last long, unless it applies only to a very limited product range. Every business has to cover its overall costs in the long run. If it does not, it will make losses, accumulate debts and will soon have to close down.

Risks

So what makes a business want to produce and sell its product? Although we have seen that motivations vary, the marketplace is actually very brutal. No matter what their motives, people in business cannot afford to make losses for long. First they must cover all of their costs so they can pay the employees, the rent and the costs of other inputs. But business is often risky. Entrepreneurs usually invest their own money in their businesses, not to mention a great deal of time. They need to be rewarded in the form of income for their own needs and compensation for the risks they are taking. A key question for them will be how much **profit** they can make, initially just to make a living. If they want to expand, profits will have to contribute to the costs of future expansion. Profit is the difference between **sales revenue** and costs of production.

Profit

> **Costs** are all the payments that have to be made in order to get a product into the market place. They will include wages, premises and all other input costs – raw materials, components, inputs bought from wholesalers, business rates, interest, energy bills and so on.
>
> **Sales Revenue = Price x Quantity Sold**
>
> **Profit = Sales Revenue – Costs of Production**
>
> **Investment** means spending now in order to generate income in the future, i.e. investing in capital equipment such as machinery, computers or vans, researching and developing the product, or training key people.

Scarcity

People who want to set up a business are looking for a gap in the market. They might consider setting up a convenience store where the nearest supermarket is over a mile away. They might create a completely new product, or they might look to do what other competing businesses are doing, but do it better or for a lower price. They are looking for a product that has some scarcity value – something about it that will make people want to pay for it. The more useful or attractive the product is, the more they will be able to charge for it. And the more they can charge, the bigger the profit will be.

Incentives

The prospect of profit provides an **incentive** to go to all the trouble of setting up a business, or expanding an existing one. The higher the price, the greater the incentive to **supply** the product. Often, entrepreneurs are comparing possibilities, looking to decide which product offers the best incentive.

Horticulture

Frank Taylor used to grow chrysanthemums in glass houses. He had a crafty system that could heat and light his glass houses so that the plants thought it was summer when it wasn't, or use blackout to put the plants in darkness, fooling them into producing flowers all year round. For a long time he made a reasonable living from this. Then many Dutch growers invested in bigger glasshouses and used their low-cost North Sea gas to heat them so they could grow flowers more cheaply. Frank couldn't match their prices and had to close down his business. He put the glasshouses on the market and eventually sold them at a rather low price to Peter Thomas, who had an idea he thought might work.

Peter wanted to grow high quality herbs and vegetables both in and out of season and supply them to high-class restaurants and smart food halls like Harrods and Selfridges in London's West End. Eight years after starting he is making a living. If he can find a few more customers he can expand because he isn't yet using all the space he has.

Do this

Using all of the words below, explain what happened in the story above, in just four sentences.

The key words: market, investment, competition, supply, costs, prices, sales revenue and profit.

Supply

Markets

We have been exploring what makes businesses want to supply their product. Markets always have two groups of players. On one side of the market there are businesses supplying products. On the other there are customers who want to buy them. These customers create the demand for the product. The more suppliers there are for any particular product, the more competitive the market will be. The more customers there are, the better the chances for the suppliers to make a profit.

Scarcity refers to a situation in which people want to buy more of a product than is currently being produced.

Incentives are financial and other rewards that can induce people to behave in a certain way. For example, the prospect of profit acts as an incentive that encourages businesses to produce more or to develop a new or different product.

Supply is one element in the market system. Market forces create incentives to supply particular types of product that customers want. The more scarce the product is, the higher the price and the profit will be when supplying it.

Demand refers to the other element in the market system, the amount of a product that customers want to buy. This will vary with the price: if it is high, there will be fewer customers.

Creating a new market

One good way to find a market is to create one by coming up with an innovative product. The late Steve Jobs did this with Apple's iPad. Tablet computers had already been invented but they were cumbersome and lacking in user-friendliness. Effectively, Apple redesigned the product so that it worked for a wide range of people. It created a market and the me-too products arrived soon after, providing competition.

Innovation

Some products don't have much of a market. Take spaceships for example. There may be many people who would like to own one and take their friends on trips into outer space. But the cost of manufacturing space ships is currently too high for there to be many potential buyers.

> Richard Branson is trying to create a business which would offer trips into space. His specially built aircraft, White Knight, will carry his Space Ship into space. Various celebrities have put down their deposits for brief flights currently priced at US$200,000. Branson isn't quite there yet, but he may be in the market by the time you read this. He's banking on the idea that if he can supply the product, there will be some people out there who can afford to buy the product and will want to as well.

Innovation can be much less complicated than this. However, using new technologies can create many opportunities for businesses. They may use them to create and supply new products. Or they may produce existing products in a more efficient way, thus reducing costs and perhaps also prices, and so increasing sales revenue.

"This is a real technological breakthrough"

Factors that affect supply

We have shown that popular products sell for good prices and create an incentive to supply the product. But there are other important influences too. Rising costs of production may mean that prices have to rise; this may cause customers to buy less of the product. Inevitably, the business will have to reduce output.

Influencing supply

Technology is enormously important and not just because it leads to the creation of new products. It frequently leads to costs being cut as more efficient production methods are developed. This means that prices can be reduced, sales will increase and more will be supplied. The process may open up a mass market.

Factors affecting supply: prices	A good price is an incentive to businesses to supply more. *Expectations* of good prices in the future will also encourage supply.
Other important factors:	*Costs of production* may change: they may push prices up or down. *New technologies* may mean costs and prices fall. Supply will rise. *Government policies* – e.g. a change in VAT or new regulations.

Supply and demand

These two market forces together determine price in a competitive market place. The next chapter examines demand and the ways in which it interacts with supply to influence prices.

Do this

On your own, quickly make a list of the ten most important products that you either want or need.

Next, swap lists with someone else's. Are they the same? If not, how and why do they differ? Talk this over.

Now, go back to your own list and write down ten more things that you want or need.

Looking at the twenty items, which of these would you buy more of if the price were lower? If the price rose, which would you buy less of (or none at all)?

Your **demand** for these products will be affected by the price you have to pay to get them.

Choice

Needs and wants are different. Needs are unavoidable – you need to eat. Wants are different in that you have some **choice** about them – you can choose between a pizza and a burger. But you can see that in both cases, choices will be affected by the amount of money you can spend.

When there are people in the market place who want to buy the things they need and want, there is demand for a wide range of products. Whether these products are needed or wanted is unimportant – either way, there will be a demand for them. The level of demand will be affected by many different factors. First and foremost, price will matter, often a great deal. If the price of asparagus is high, relatively few people will buy it. Many will buy carrots or beans instead.

> **Demand** refers to the quantity of a product that will be bought at a range of specific prices.
>
> **Choice** – because resources are scarce, everyone has to choose what they want most, in light of the price they will have to pay for it. Choice will be constrained by the level of income – the amount that the consumer can spend.

Price

Have you ever watched someone trying to sell their home? It might go easily, or it might not. Sometimes the seller gets the asking price fairly soon after putting their home on the market. (The estate agent might say that they had priced the property realistically.) Other times, few people show any interest. The seller may decide to get a new agent or advertise more widely. But the action that is most likely to achieve a sale would be to reduce the asking price, or show willingness to negotiate. While there may be no demand for the property at the higher price, potential buyers will materialise if the price is lower.

Selling a house may require a reduction in the asking price.

Price is not the only factor

Non-price factors

A different angle

A company has designed a new chocolate bar which is different from all the others. It combines the chunkiness of a Yorkie with the crunchiness of a Crunchie and the chewiness of a Snickers. It seems to meet the needs of all the consumers of chocolate bars that the marketing department has talked with. But will it sell?

- List the reasons why you might buy a chocolate bar.
- What might you buy? When are you likely to buy it? Where are you likely to buy it? Rank the factors influencing your choice of chocolate bar, from the most to least important.
- Compare your ideas with someone else's. What are the similarities and differences in your answers?
- What factors might influence the demand for chocolate bars: (a) for the whole of your group and (b) for a group of working adults.

Questions

1. Explain how the price might affect your decision.
2. Assuming the price was similar to those of other chocolate bars, what will be the key factors determining whether a sale takes place?

Important as price is in influencing demand, i.e. the quantities that consumers want to buy, there are other factors to consider.

Tastes

- For some products, personal **tastes** will be an important influence on sales. If the new chocolate bar really is as interesting as it sounds, it may appeal to many people. They will buy it if they like it better than the competing alternatives. **Fashions** are also very relevant, though perhaps not with chocolate. Advertising can affect demand – in fact, increasing demand for the product is its main objective. It works by changing tastes and encouraging fashions. This may affect the demand for competing products as well as the advertised product.

Incomes

- **Incomes** can also be very important. If many people have lost their jobs lately, and others are worried that they might too, many people will try to spend less. They may concentrate on needs rather than wants and chocolate bars may be affected. Rising incomes often help to increase demand for high-priced items such as cars and exotic holidays.

Substitutes

Complements

- Prices of other goods can have a significant effect. The key factor here is the availability of **substitutes**. If the price of one product rises, consumers will be likely to switch to a similar competing product for which the price has stayed the same. An increase in petrol prices could lead to more people travelling by train; smaller quantities of petrol would be demanded and the demand for train tickets would increase. Less often, prices of **complements** may have an impact. Parking is sometimes a complement for cars and petrol. The price of parking space in many attractive places has increased lately. This leads to less petrol being bought as some people will go by train or bus or use the park and ride facility.

Differing circumstances

So far we have assumed that falling incomes mean a fall in demand and therefore in sales. This is normal – and the products concerned are sometimes called **normal goods**. But there are some very obvious exceptions to this normality. Sometimes when incomes are falling, people switch from a dearer to a cheaper product and the latter sells far better than before. The cheaper product is called an **inferior good**, meaning that it sells well when incomes are causing people to rethink their buying habits and going for something cheaper.

The number of visitors to Brighton rose during the period 2008-10, even though incomes were falling for many people. The trains from London were packed on Saturday mornings. Many people were having days out because they were afraid of losing their jobs and did not want to take expensive holidays. Domino's Pizza did well at that time too.

Influences on demand

Substitutes are products that can be used to replace each other. So if the price of one rises, the demand for the other will rise. The vast majority of products have substitutes and competition between them is often an important element in the level of demand for any one of them.

Complements are used together, so if the price of one rises, the demand for the other will fall. In practice the changes may be quite small but we can always show the direction of the change.

Inferior goods are those which people buy more of when their incomes fall. Products that are not inferior are called **normal goods**.

Factors affecting demand: *prices*	When prices fall people generally buy more of the product
	Changes in taxes, e.g. on petrol, or a change in VAT, may affect prices
Other important factors:	*Incomes*
	Price and availability of *substitutes*
	Price and availability of *complements*
	Tastes and fashions – which may be affected by *advertising*
	Population – increases demand if it is growing.

It is worth remembering that sometimes, substitutes can be quite different products. For example, you might well find that you have a choice between a new car and an exotic holiday. If air fares rise, you might decide that you would do better to buy the car instead. It is not in itself going to give you a holiday but it may provide better value enjoyment.

Show what you know

In each of the following situations, explain what would happen and why. *(See warning overleaf.)*

A change occurs:	What is or was the impact on:
The fashion for fur-lined boots took off	The price of fur-lined boots
	The quantity demanded of other kinds of footwear
Increasing numbers of people take skiing holidays	The demand for ski clothes and equipment
Managers of some very big businesses got increasingly large bonuses	The number of people signing up for Virgin's space travel
The Tata Nano (a very cheap car) is launched in the UK market	Sales of other cars in the UK
An advertising campaign is used to launch an innovative vacuum cleaner	Sales of this and other brands of vacuum cleaner

> ### ⚠ WATCH OUT!
>
> When you are answering questions, be careful to make best possible use of the jargon – the words that are given very specific meanings in the subject you are studying. So for the above questions, it would be important to include terms like substitute, complement, competing and market, as well as the obvious ones like price, incomes, tastes and fashions. Students often forget to use the jargon and miss valuable opportunities to demonstrate their understanding.

Supply and demand interact

In any market, you will find that supply and demand interact with one another continuously. A change of any kind will lead to repercussions. Some markets are changing all the time – petrol prices change quite often, maybe depending on political events in the countries that are large-scale producers. Other markets are much more stable with only occasional changes.

Market changes

In Chapter 4 you looked at the way rising prices might create an incentive to supply more of the product. Think about the situation where a sudden fashion has created increased demand for, say, scooters. Retailers can charge quite high prices for them because many people want to buy them. This high price creates a bigger incentive and the producers will immediately expand output as fast as they can. Later, when most people who want a scooter have got one, competition will cause the price to slip back down again.

Similarly when clothing fashions change, retailers will end up selling the unwanted products at discounted sale prices, and these lines of production will look very unprofitable to suppliers. Rather than make a loss they will either cut production or discontinue the product altogether. There is a disincentive to produce. Both quantity supplied and quantity demanded will change.

The quantity supplied responds to changes in demand which which cause prices and profits to increase or decrease.

The quantity demanded responds to changes in prices as consumers try to get the best value for the amount they spend.

What happens when incomes are rising world-wide and car sales increase? In fast-growing economies like China and India, incomes are rising. Many people want cars and now they can pay for them. (In 2011, Jaguar Land Rover sold 70% more cars in China than in 2010.) But of course, to run the cars more petrol is needed. The flow chart traces each stage of the changes that take place and explains how the supply of oil is affected.

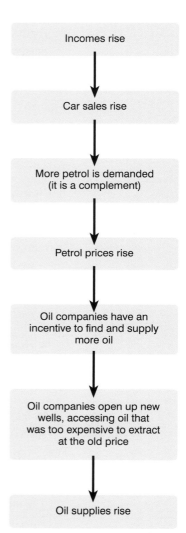

Incomes rise

↓

Car sales rise

↓

More petrol is demanded (it is a complement)

↓

Petrol prices rise

↓

Oil companies have an incentive to find and supply more oil

↓

Oil companies open up new wells, accessing oil that was too expensive to extract at the old price

↓

Oil supplies rise

When car sales rise more petrol is demanded.

What will influence supply?

In Chapter 4 we found that prices affect the quantity supplied because they make the product either more or less profitable and create an incentive to produce more or less. But supply can change for other reasons too:

- Costs of production
- Technical change.

Prices and costs

When **costs of production** fall, businesses can cut their prices and still make enough profit to survive. Where there is competition, falling prices will bring more customers into the market and sales will rise. Think about TVs. To start with, long ago in the 1950s, they were expensive. But as technologies improved and producers became more experienced, prices fell until in time, thirty years later, nearly everyone had a TV. There has been a similar story with many new products, more recently with smartphones and flat screen TVs. Most producers look to sell at high prices at first, to just a few people (the early adopters). This helps them to recoup the development costs of the product. Later they aim for the mass market, using the experience they have gained to produce more cheaply. As the price falls the quantity demanded can increase dramatically.

Technological change

Technological change allows dynamic businesses to produce completely new products, as well as to find new, cheaper ways of producing that cut costs. These are called respectively, **product innovation** and **process innovation**.

Innovation

> **Costs of production** are all those payments that are needed in order to create a product and make it available in the market. They include wages, the cost of premises and capital equipment and the cost of any bought-in inputs like components in a car factory or shampoo at the hairdressers.
>
> **Product innovation** refers to the development of completely new products.
>
> **Process innovation** uses new technologies to produce existing or similar products at lower cost.
>
> **Technical or technological change** uses new scientific knowledge and improved engineering techniques to create both new products and new production methods.

Show your understanding

For each of the following situations, draw a flow chart like the one on page 28 that includes each change in the market as supply and demand interact. Don't forget the possible consequences for competing substitutes. N.B. some flow charts will be longer than others.

Dyson comes up with another new type of vacuum cleaner and advertises it widely.

Leggings go out of fashion.

The cost of making iPads falls as improvements are made to the technologies involved.

Doctors recommend massage as a way of reducing stress and improving health.

A combination of rising population and rising incomes increases demand for food worldwide.

Market orientation

Businesses that are slow to respond to market changes tend to run into trouble. Sales revenue will fall as customers turn away to competing products. Profits will fall and turn to losses and they may have to make some employees redundant. In thinking through the choices they have, pleasing the customers will have to be given a high priority.

Studying the market

In the case study on page 26, the marketing department at the chocolate makers' had been busy finding out what people would like. Many businesses try market testing, seeing how customers get on with the new product in a small area, and making improvements that increase the chances of customer enthusiasm. Section 1.3.3, Evaluating a business opportunity, looks at these ideas in more detail (pages 37-61).

The businesses that are nimble and adaptable when markets change are likely to be the most profitable and successful in terms of sales. They will be the best able to spot opportunities for new and improved products (product innovation) and to adopt new ways of producing (process innovation).

Market orientation contrasts with product orientation. This describes the situation where the business is primarily concerned with the product rather than the market. Management concentrates on perfecting the product, rather than finding out whether it is what the customers actually want.

Market orientation in decision-making implies that the business will focus on the needs of the customer before taking decisions about the product, its price and the way it is promoted.

Product orientation implies that the business will focus its efforts on creating the product rather than responding to market preferences.

Think

Identify two businesses that you think are brilliantly market oriented. Then share your thoughts with someone else and compare and contrast their choices with yours.

Chapter 6

Supply and demand interacting: some diagrams

> ⚠️ **WARNING**
>
> This chapter is all about how you can analyse the interaction of supply and demand using diagrams. It is perfectly possible to get full marks for exam questions on supply and demand without drawing a diagram. Diagrams are not required except in Unit 2b and you may not be taking that Unit at all. However, your teacher may well think that diagrams actually make it easier to understand and explain how supply and demand interact. If that applies to you, then this chapter will be helpful. The first two pages of this chapter cover diagrams that are fairly easy to grasp.

Eateries

Late in 2011, Harry Ramsden, the famous chain of classy fish and chip shops, had to close its original 83-year old restaurant. Demand was slowing; the chain was running at a loss. At the time, many people had experienced falling incomes. Yet pizza, burger and burrito chains were flourishing. Domino's Pizza and McDonalds were doing well and Wagamama's was still looking to set up new outlets. Domino's Pizza had been particularly successful. It had been very active in advertising, distributing millions of inserts in periodicals and offering discounts on multiple purchases.

Discussion points

(a) Explain how the businesses in this story might have been affected by falling incomes.

(b) Why do you think Harry Ramsden got into trouble when it did?

Constructing a demand curve

On page 26, we looked at the way the number of chocolate bars demanded might be affected by price. Refresh your memory about the story and then estimate the likely demand yourselves. Draw up a table like the one below. First fill in column 2 for yourself and then pool your results with those of a few other people and write them into column 3. (If one person has an opinion which is extreme, in comparison to the group, leave this out of the total for now.)

Demand and price

Price of a chocolate bar	Number you would buy	Number the group would buy
60p		
70p		
80p		
90p		
£1.00		
£1.10		
£1.20		

Next, draw a graph. Put price on the vertical (x) axis and quantity on the horizontal (y) axis. Plot the group quantity demanded at each price. No surprises: as the price falls, quantity demanded increases. **Demand curves** slope downwards to the right. In normal circumstances all demand curves look roughly like this.

**Supply
and price**

Now let's think about the supply of chocolate bars. If the product is selling fast, the strong demand will push the price up and create an incentive for the manufacturers to expand output. We can't produce a **supply curve** for ourselves in the way we can with a demand curve. But we know that as prices rise, producers are going to want to create and sell more to take advantage of the incentive. So the supply curve is usually going to start low down on the left where incentives are very unpromising in terms of potential profit, and slope upwards to the right.

Hint: Demand down, supply to the sky.

Equilibrium price

Equilibrium

Figure 6.1 shows how supply and demand intersect to determine the price at which both consumers and producers will be satisfied. We call this the **equilibrium price**.

Figure 6.1: Equilibrium price

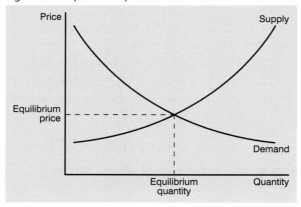

**Market
clearing**

This equilibrium price is sometimes called the **market clearing price**. There will be no unsold stocks of the product lying uselessly in the warehouse. There will be no dissatisfied consumers finding that the shop has sold out of the product they had set their hearts on buying. The market clears.

The **demand curve** shows the relationship between price and the quantity that customers want to buy. A demand curve can be produced for individuals but is normally used to show the total demand for all the customers who are in the market for the product, at a range of different prices.

The **supply curve** shows the relationship between the price and the quantity that producers want to create and sell. It shows the total amount supplied to the market by all producers of that product, at a range of prices.

The **equilibrium price** is the price at which both buyers and sellers will be satisfied, in that the amount that producers wish to sell is the same as the amount that customers want to buy.

The **market clearing price** is the price at which all of the product that is currently available sells, and no one who wanted to buy the product at the going price fails to get it.

When the price is above or below the market clearing price problems develop. People who are trying to sell their homes at a good price may find that they do not sell. Market traders who charge too much will have unsold stocks at the end of the day. Manufacturers may finish up with surplus stocks. If the price is too low, some customers may be disappointed because the product was unavailable by the time they got to the shop – there was a shortage. We call this disequilibrium.

Market change

Market forces

Many markets are quite stable and prices are steady over long periods. Other markets are not like that at all; they are volatile, constantly changing to create a restless scenario where prices are never still. The stock exchange – the market for company shares – is like this. So is the foreign exchange market where different currencies are traded. In contrast, the restaurant and takeaway chains in the case study above are in a more stable market. There will not be swift day-to-day changes but prices and quantities sold will vary as market forces influence demand and supply.

Market change can affect almost any activity. Copper prices shot up in 2011, because Chinese building programmes required copper piping in increasing quantities. It takes time to find and start up new copper mines so the first thing that happened was that the price rose. If this continues, there will be an incentive to find and exploit new sources of the metal ore. But in the meantime, copper prices are very volatile and depend on how much demand there is at any particular time.

Show your understanding

Looking at the list of products below, allocate each to one of three groups – either tending to be stable, tending to be volatile, or normally stable but subject to change in response to specific events. Then explain what specific events might affect prices for each one. Discuss your conclusions with others who are thinking about this.

Wheat, flats and houses, car insurance, plain T-shirts, crude oil, business software programs, lace tights, care homes.

Constructing diagrams

A shift in the demand curve

Figure 6.2

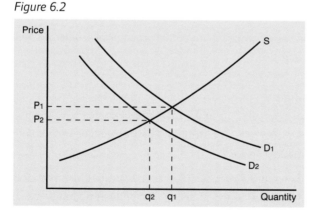

Returning to the restaurant chains, these market changes are mainly about demand. Do we want more fish and chips or more pizzas? Demand for these products is much affected by personal tastes and preferences. Clearly, these were shifting away from the traditional fish and chip meal: people wanted fewer of them. **The demand curve was shifting to the left.** At each and every price a smaller quantity would be demanded. Figure 6.2 shows the effects. The flow chart traces the sequence of events.

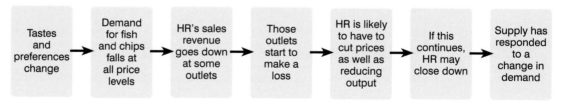

Harry Ramsden could have considered cutting prices. This would make it more competitive with substitute eateries. However, it is clear from the story that the business preferred to close its loss-making outlets and concentrate on those that were profitable.

Is the change in tastes the only reason why Harry Ramsden is in trouble? Probably not. After 2008, many economies, including the UK, were either in recession (output falling) or stagnant (output growing very

Fewer Indian chefs are available because of government immigration policy, putting up the costs of production in Indian restaurants.

Different markets

slowly). Many people lost their jobs and some were unemployed for some time. Many experienced falling or slow-growing incomes and were nervous about the future. One thing people can always cut back on is meals out and takeaways. Falling incomes could have been a factor for Harry Ramsden. Figure 6.2 would work perfectly well to explain the effect of falling incomes.

It is possible that Harry Ramsden's products are normal goods while Domino's Pizza is an inferior good. (Check the definitions on pages 26-27.)

Show your understanding

1. Construct a flow chart to show each stage of the process that was affecting Domino's at the same time as Harry Ramsden was in difficulty. (See the opening case study and the follow up information on page 33 and above.)

2. Draw a supply and demand diagram which shows what happened to Domino's Pizza. Then explain why its experience in a period of falling incomes was quite different from that of Harry Ramsden's.

3. Draw a demand and supply diagram that shows what happens to the demand curve for small, economical cars when the price of petrol rises. What will happen to the price of small cars and the quantity sold?

Hint: It can be useful to illustrate an exam answer with a supply and demand diagram. But it must be fully and correctly labelled, and referred to in your explanation.

Changes in supply

Some Indian restaurants have been struggling recently. Indian cuisine is more complicated than some competing takeaway products like pizzas and burgers, and requires more experienced chefs. In its efforts

Rising costs

to curb immigration, the UK government restricted the number of visas it gives for chefs from India, Pakistan and Bangladesh. These immigrant chefs have been both experienced and willing to work for quite low pay. With fewer of them available, the restaurants have found it hard to keep their prices competitive. In effect, their costs of production have risen because the availability of chefs willing to work for low pay has been restricted and training is costly.

When costs rise, **the supply curve shifts upwards**. Any given quantity of the product will cost more to produce. Producers will want to raise prices to cover the extra costs. Obviously the reverse will happen when costs fall.

Figure 6.3: A rise in costs of production

A shift in the supply curve

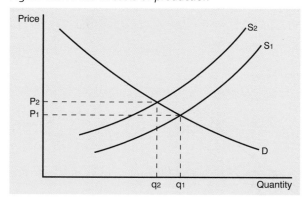

Show your understanding

1. Figure 6.3 shows the effect of reducing the number of immigrant chefs from the Indian sub-continent. What happens to the price and quantity sold of Indian meals?

2. Draw a supply and demand diagram to show what happens in the market for iPads as further technological developments reduce costs of production. Explain the effect on price and quantity sold.

Eric Pickles, the government's community secretary, who himself enjoys chicken tikka, has plans to set up a 'curry school'. The idea is that chefs will be trained here in the UK. No one knows whether this will help the suppliers of Indian food to get through the recession without making a loss.

> ⚠ **WARNING**
>
> Be careful with statements like demand is rising, or supply is decreasing. Let's use demand as the example. 'Demand is rising' could mean one of two things.
>
> - The price has fallen, encouraging the quantity demanded to rise. There has been a *movement along the demand curve*.
>
> - Or, at all prices, the quantity demanded has increased. This would be a *shift in the demand curve*, to the right. It could be the result of rising incomes, or a new fashion for the product, or a fall in the price of a substitute.
>
> You must try hard to show exactly what you mean when you say demand has increased. Similarly, a change in supply could be the result of a change in price, i.e. a movement along the supply curve, or it could be the result of a change in costs of production or in the technologies used (which itself would alter costs). This would involve a shift in the supply curve.

Shifts in and movements along...

Getting the analysis right

> **Hint:** whenever there is a change in price, the quantity moves along the curve. Any change other than price will shift the curve.

When technical improvements are made to the production process, costs of production fall. This means that the same quantity or more can be produced more cheaply. The supply curve shifts downwards. This could happen if the oil companies find new and cheaper ways of reaching oil in places that are technically difficult to reach.

Figure 6.4 shows how this works. The oil companies can reduce the price of oil, and sell more. There is a movement along the demand curve and a shift in the supply curve, showing the fall in price and the rising quantity.

Figure 6.4: The effect of falling costs

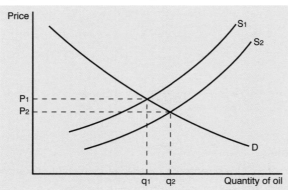

Do this

Draw your own diagram showing what happened when a health campaign caused more people to take out membership at fitness centres, regardless of the price. Where is the movement and where is the shift? What consequences might the change have for price and quantity sold?

Hint: never try to put more than one change at a time on your diagram. If there are two possible changes, draw a separate diagram for each. Practise drawing diagrams for a wide range of different real world situations.

Chapter 7

Researching demand for the business idea

Car parking

Dan's parents weren't particularly green fingered and throughout his childhood they had always increased his pocket money if he mowed the front lawn and kept the plants tidy. Dan could command *double* pocket money: his parents' lawn was huge! It was so big, in fact, that Dan used to have a full five-a-side game of football on it with nine friends, with ease.

Dan loved his football and was delighted when his team, Brighton and Hove Albion, decided to move from their temporary home, the Withdean Stadium, to a new ground just outside the town. The new ground was nearer to Dan's home but it wasn't the shorter journey to home games that pleased Dan; it had given him a business idea.

Tired of doing the lawn but not wanting to give up the income it generated for him, he tried to persuade his parents to cover it all in gravel. Where would the income come from? Charging football fans to park on it on match day!

Dan's parents told Dan that he could start his enterprise if he could prove that it would work. He waited for the first few games of the season to see how the traffic and parking situation was working out. Dan saw that the council had put double yellow lines on the local roads and car parks were often full by midday for a 3pm kick off. Encouraged, he went to an 'Albion internet forum' and asked if people thought that home and away fans would be interested in paying £5 for parking on his drive. The response was remarkable. Dan did one quick check that the council or the club weren't planning on extending their car parks and presented his findings to his parents. The gravel arrived the next day.

Discussion points

(a) How did research help Dan develop his business idea?

(b) What risks would Dan have faced if he hadn't conducted any research?

(c) What other research might Dan have had to conduct if he wasn't a football fan himself?

Market research

A new product

Starting a business, or launching a new product in an established business, both involve significant up-front costs. These include:

- product development
- investment in equipment and premises to produce the product or provide the service
- spending on initial marketing.

Businesses try to ensure that these potentially expensive outlays carry the minimal possible risk. In order to do this they conduct **market research**, which is the process of finding out information about customers, competitors and market conditions. Gathering this information will allow them to be more confident that investing in the new idea will be profitable in the long term.

The table below shows how market research can reduce risk when developing a new business idea:

Purpose – allows the entrepreneur to:	Procedure
• quantify potential demand	Using the results of market research, entrepreneurs can forecast future sales. This allows them to estimate future sales revenue and decide whether it will cover the costs of production.
• understand how much customers are willing to pay	An entrepreneur can assess whether the price that people want to pay will be sufficient to cover costs of production.
• understand customer behaviour	Entrepreneurs can work out how best to interact with the consumer. This will include finding out exactly who the product appeals to and why, so that they can sell it in the right places and advertise it and promote it in a way that will be effective with those people. It may also highlight a customer craving for a product or service that is currently unavailable; this will give the entrepreneur an incentive to explore the possibility of meeting these customer needs.
• identify competitors and their unique selling points (USPs)	The entrepreneur can ensure that their own business idea is able to compete effectively with existing businesses by having a source of competitive advantage which makes it stand out from competitors.
• identify key features of the business environment	The entrepreneur can decide whether social, legal, economic, political and technological (SLEPT) factors are favourable to the successful launch of the new business idea.

Market research (margin label)

Types of market research

Secondary research (margin label)

A lot of the questions that businesses may ask about the issues surrounding their new idea may have already been answered by other organisations. Interrogating these data sources is known as **secondary** or **desk research**. This name comes from the fact that the information is 'second hand' to the business that is using it. Researchers can simply review it from their desks in the office.

Primary research (margin label)

When the business can't find answers to their questions from an existing source, they will carry out their own research, known as **primary** or **field research**. This name comes from the fact the information is found out 'in the field'. The researchers will be looking directly at the market and the information they collect is 'first hand' to the person doing it.

> **Market research** is the process of gathering data in order to understand current and future customer needs and factors affecting the marketplace. This reduces the risks associated with developing a new business idea.
>
> **Primary market research** is obtained 'first hand' by the business that is interested in the results. It involves fieldwork and can be directly related to the needs of the individual business. Also known as field research.

Secondary market research uses data that has been gathered previously by another organisation and is publicly available. Also known as desk research.

Different approaches to primary research

Market research can also be categorised in another way, according to the type of data collected. If the outcomes of the research are numerical, such as quantities or percentages, it is known as **quantitative research**. This might generate estimates of future sales or preferred shopping habits and times, or the size, qualities, features and colours of an ideal product.

Other kinds of data might require **qualitative research**. It could concern the psychology of the potential customers – their opinions or feelings about the product. This kind of data cannot be put into numbers. But it can reveal much about consumer attitudes and behaviour, their perceptions and their anxieties.

Quantitative market research – market research conducted where the results are numerical and can be analysed statistically.

Qualitative market research – market research conducted where the results are based on opinions and feelings.

Both primary and secondary research can be either quantitative or qualitative. Good market research will link qualitative and quantitative data to build a detailed picture of the customers' preferences.

Ways of conducting market research

Primary methods	How they can be used
Questionnaire/survey	Asking people a pre-planned set of open and closed questions to gather qualitative and quantitative data respectively.
	Questionnaires can be used for postal or phone surveys, or in personal interviews. They must be very carefully designed and should be clear, relevant, logically sequenced and never personally intrusive. In general, closed-end questions give a choice of answers and provide quantitative data. Open-ended questions provide individual answers that yield qualitative information.
	Comment: this could be very detailed, or could consist of asking a few friends or colleagues to answer two or three simple questions about an idea
Focus group	Assembling people for a group discussion on a topic led by the researcher. The nature of the research means the data is always qualitative and attempts to capture the perceptions, reactions and attitude of the group to a product, service or advertisement. For example, a group might be asked what they think of a planned advertisement or change in branding, or about their attitude to a competitor, in order to refine the business idea or plan a rival product that exploits their weaknesses.
	Comment: running a focus group really well requires specialist skills. Entrepreneurs may need to hire a market research company to do this so it can be an expensive strategy. Some small businesses may not be able to afford this type of market research, especially when starting up.

Quantitative or qualitative

Primary research

	Observation	Watching and studying the actions of potential customers, suppliers and competitors. This can include:
		• counting the footfall (including the type of person) walking past a prospective retail site in order to assess the suitability of the location
		• observing how customers move around the store in order to learn how to position products for better sales
		• studying the product range or pricing of a competitor to spot a potential gap in the market (see Chapter 8).
		• gathering information on the shortfalls of another product or service, in order to spot a gap in the market.
		Comment: This can be quite quick and simple for an entrepreneur without specialist marketing skills. It is also generally cost-free.
Test marketing	Test marketing	Launching a product in a small portion of the market (normally a limited geographical location) and evaluating the response to it. This may be done to avoid the costs of a 'national' launch before the product is proven. (See Chapter 10, page 60.)
		Comment: an entrepreneur might do very small scale test marketing by, for example, asking friends to try a new recipe (for a bakery) or providing a free service in return for detailed feedback (e.g. Tamara, in Chapter 2, may have given her friends free massages in order to test out new techniques).

	Secondary methods	**How they can be used**
Secondary research	Market reports	Organisations such as Mintel and Key Note produce reports on trends in the market, which are available for purchase by businesses. They will inform about changes in consumer attitudes and how established businesses are responding to these changes.
	Government data	National and local government provide details on the demographics of the population. For example it will be relatively easy to find out the age, gender or income distribution of people in a certain area.
Forecasting	Economic historic and forecast data	Trends in unemployment, economic growth, inflation and consumer spending are available from governmental and non-governmental sources. This data will be useful, particularly if sales of the product are dependent on strong consumer confidence.
	Internet	Search engines make it easy to find out if there is any competition in the market that a business is considering entering. Furthermore, services like Google Maps allow researchers to plot the locations of competitors in a geographical area.
	Trade publications	Lots of industries have specialist magazines that report on trends in the market. For example, *The Grocer* and *Hotelier* report on trends in the grocery and hospitality market respectively and will give insight to new businesses on customer needs and how they are currently being met.

Which method is best?

There is no simple answer to this question as it depends entirely on the situation. This is because primary and secondary research both have their own distinctive advantages and disadvantages. In reality many businesses find that a combination of methods works best, with primary research following some secondary research that can contribute useful background information. The entrepreneur needs to balance three key issues: cost, time and ease of data collection.

Costs vs. accuracy

	Primary research	Secondary research
Advantages	• Is certainly up to date as it is conducted as required • Can be exactly tailored to the needs of the business • Can produce data which competitors do not have access to.	• Is available immediately and often relatively inexpensively (or free), compared to carrying out costly primary research from scratch.
Disadvantages	• Can be expensive to carry out • Can be time consuming to carry out and interpret • Some methods such as focus groups can require specialist skills • Interviewer bias may be a problem	• May be out of date • Difficult to guarantee accuracy and reliability • Some sources can be expensive to purchase (e.g. market reports) • Data is not private so competitors can access it too.

Example

Sophie is considering setting up an upmarket restaurant. She is interested in the income level in the local area, so she can estimate how many people would have the disposable income to eat out regularly. This will help her to quantify demand. Sophie would like to conduct a survey of the incomes of all local residents, but it would be incredibly time consuming to do this for even a local area, even if people were willing to share the information. For this reason she may decide to use secondary research conducted by the local council. Although it may not be exactly what she is looking for, Sophie is willing to trade off accuracy against time needed.

If Sophie is satisfied that there are enough people in the local area with good incomes that will sustain a restaurant, she might carry out some primary research. This will help her to decide what pricing strategies might be most successful with the potential customers.

There would be little point in researching pricing strategies if secondary research showed there weren't enough customers. This shows why it is often best to use free or cheap secondary research first, to validate the basic idea before committing to the time and expense of doing primary research to test the idea fully.

Exam question practice

1. Explain two reasons why an entrepreneur would conduct market research before launching a new product. *(6 marks)*

2. Analyse two benefits of carrying out primary research to an entrepreneur planning to expand their business into a new location. *(8 marks)*

Surveys and questionnaires can gather information from a sample of potential consumers.

Sampling

Often it isn't possible to complete research which includes *all* potential customers. For example, at the beginning of this chapter you learned about Dan – he would have found it very difficult to contact all fans of Brighton and Hove Albion, as well as all away fans who may come to a match during the year. Dan used an internet forum as a way of accessing some of the fans in his target market and then made an assumption that their opinion was a fair reflection of all of the fans in the market. Dan used a *sample* (the fans who responded) to make judgements about the whole *population* (all fans).

Surveys and questionnaires

Market research often involves **sampling**, particularly where quantitative primary research is required. Sampling is much quicker and easier than trying to collect data from a whole population. Surveys and questionnaires can gather information from a sample of potential consumers. The sample size must be large enough to reflect the variations in people's responses reasonably accurately. In general, the larger a sample, the more confident we can be that it will represent the whole population. An entrepreneur faces a trade-off between accuracy (larger is better) and cost/time (smaller is better) when deciding on the size of a sample.

Potential bias

The people in the sample must be selected carefully, otherwise It may have a **bias** towards one particular group. Standing in a shopping place during working hours and asking passers-by for an interview will definitely produce a biased sample because it will include a larger percentage of retired and unemployed people than that existing in the population as a whole. This can be called a *convenience sample* as the researcher questions people who happen to be nearby. This might provide very unhelpful results if you wanted to know about customer preferences for an expensive new game. There are a number of techniques for selecting a sample which can help to avoid bias:

Random samples

- A **random sample** could be made representative of the population by taking, say, every 100th name from the electoral register. This can be expensive: it might involve visiting people at their homes several times, before finding them in and willing to answer questions. It might also take a lot of time to travel to different locations.

Sample types

● An alternative would be a **quota sample**. Using this method, a researcher ensures that responses from different groups of individuals accurately reflect the distribution of those groups in the population as a whole. So there would be representative groups distinguished according to age, gender, occupation and perhaps other factors too. The researcher would make sure to interview the required number of each group in order to get a certain percentage of each type of respondent in the sample.

● Another alternative is **stratified sampling**, which means selecting from a particular segment of the population. For example, Sophie (page 41) might try to interview only people who looked relatively prosperous, since the less well off people in the neighbourhood probably couldn't afford her prices.

Sampling involves collecting data from a group of people who will be representative of the target market or the population as a whole.

Bias occurs when information collected from a sample does not accurately reflect variations in the total population. This is likely if the sample is small or inappropriately selected.

A **random sample** is one in which everyone has an equal chance of being selected.

A **quota sample** involves dividing the target market into groups according to their consumer characteristics; a percentage of the sample will be allocated to each group.

Stratified samples are similar to quota samples but select participants within the groups on a random basis, to gain greater accuracy.

⚠ WATCH OUT!

Market research is often much more sophisticated than just doing questionnaires. In fact, very little market research is done this way. Instead, a lot of research is done using observation and focus groups because it gives a much deeper understanding of the customers and the market. Also it is often possible to observe people who wouldn't be willing to fill in a questionnaire.

Case study: Apple vs. Market Research

Steve Jobs' opinions about market research are well documented. In several separate interviews he dismissed the value of market research when developing new products at Apple.

"A lot of times, people don't know what they want until you show it to them."

"You can't just ask customers what they want then try to give that to them. By the time you get it built, they'll want something new."

When asked what market research went into the iPad, Mr Jobs replied: *"None. It's not the consumers' job to know what they want."*

Meanwhile, Vicky Rogers swears by the market research she conducted when setting up Really Lovely Camping Company in 2009. Vicky had been taken on holiday to Scotland by her boyfriend for their anniversary. She was initially sceptical when she found out her boyfriend had booked to go camping until she looked at the 'tent' they were staying in. The 'tent' was actually a semi permanent geodesic fabric dome and had a log burner, a full size bed, a kitchen with a dishwasher and a 42 inch flat screen TV. Vicky quickly learned that this was 'glamping', not camping.

She returned from the holiday brimming with ideas. She was convinced that there was a market for glamping in the UK. She quickly began researching to see if there were other 'posh' glamping places in the UK by using the internet and looking at travel guides and brochures. Excited by what she didn't see, she began to research suitable sites where she could set up her own glamping experience in the Forest of Dean national park, around 50 miles away from her hometown, Worcester. Once she found a site she researched publications that were read by high income earners without children. These would become her target market so that she could advertise effectively.

Three years on the business is going from strength to strength. Looking back she says "market research gave me the confidence to go ahead with the business idea and give up my job." When asked what piece of research had been most useful, she answered without hesitation: "Finding out the level of competition, definitely. But I had no idea what media and promotion would influence my target market, so finding that out was really important too.

Questions

1. Does Steve Jobs' viewpoint suggest that Apple is product or market orientated? (See page 30, Chapter 5.) Explain your answer.

2. Do you think Vicky's trip to Scotland was market research? Explain your answer, outlining what method and type of research you think it was.

3. Identify two other methods of market research conducted by Vicky and state whether they were primary or secondary and qualitative or quantitative.

4. Explain why Vicky didn't think she needed to research future economic trends when setting up the Really Lovely Camping Company at a time when there were many people whose incomes were generally not growing.

5. Discuss the contrasting viewpoints regarding the usefulness of market research.

Do this

Create a market research plan for a business idea of your choice. Identify the research methods you would use and, for each, identify:

- The likely cost
- The resources you would need
- How you would use the data collected to help refine your business idea.

Chapter 8

Is there a market for the business idea?

iOS, Android, or Blackberry? or Windows?

Jamie left university in 2010 with a Computer Science degree and an idea.

Jamie was a talented Computer Scientist but awful in the kitchen. Like most students, Jamie spent very little time cooking because he didn't have any knowledge of recipes. His idea was to put his strength and his weakness together: create a smartphone app where you could tell it the ingredients you currently had in the house and it would provide a recipe that you could make with them.

Jamie initially thought that his primary target market would be other students. But he soon realised that there were probably thousands of people who had a fridge full of food but were not sure what they could make with it.

It was clear that this project would require many hours of development time. Jamie thought it might stop him from searching for a job. So he decided first to try working out how big the market might be for smartphone applications, and if there was potential scope for market growth in the future.

Discussion point
What information would you advise Jamie to try to find out about the smartphone applications market?

Market size

Market size can be measured in two ways:

Volume or value?

- the value of all the items sold in the market in £s
- the volume of all the items sold in the market in 000s.

Measuring by one method is not necessarily better than another. For example, it is quite feasible for the size of the market to have grown in volume (more items have been sold) but at the same time, shrunk in value because the price of each item has fallen considerably in the market. An example of this is shown in the table below where market size has grown by volume but fallen by value:

Market for Blu-Ray DVDs	Average selling price (£)	Market size (volume of items sold, 000)	Market size (value of items sold, £000)
2010	20	100	2000
2011	15	110	1650

Market share

Market leaders

The **market share** of a business is their sales (£) as a percentage of the overall market. For example, in October 2010 the UK clothing market was estimated to be worth £25.2bn. Primark's sales were £2.57bn so it had a 10.2% share of the market.

The business which has the greatest market share is called the **market leader**. In markets with very few businesses you might need 40-50% to be the market leader, but when there are lots of small firms in the market, the market leader can have a much smaller market share. For example the UK hairdressing market is made up mainly of thousands of individual salons with one or two national chains such as Toni and Guy, who will be market leaders but have a very small market share of hairdressing nationally.

Market growth

Market growth is an increase in market size, normally expressed as a percentage. Market growth indicates that demand for the product is increasing. Market growth can be rapid if the product is completely new and people want it but can be slow or static when the product is well established. Market growth will be negative when demand for the product is falling.

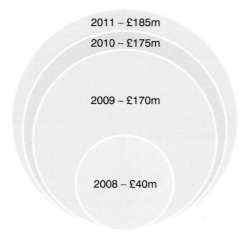

2011 – £185m

2010 – £175m

2009 – £170m

Notice, after rapid growth, the market grows much more slowly from 2010

2008 – £40m

Businesses are sometimes falsely pre-occupied with market share when they should be looking at market growth. A business can have an increasing market share but actually be receiving less sales revenue if the market is experiencing negative growth. This is shown diagrammatically below:

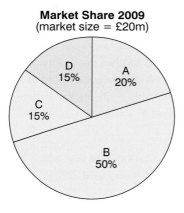

Market Share 2009
(market size = £20m)

D 15%
A 20%
C 15%
B 50%

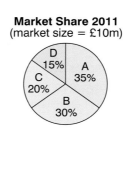

Market Share 2011
(market size = £10m)

D 15%
A 35%
C 20%
B 30%

Over two years business A has grown its market share by 15% (mostly at the expense of business B) but in that time the market has halved in size. Therefore, despite an increase in market share, revenues have actually fallen. Business B has presumably reduced its commitment to this market (given its fall in size) and set up in a new one.

Market share

Market size is measured either by the total value or the total volume of goods sold in the market.

Market share is shown by the percentage of the market that the individual business sells to.

Market growth is an increase in the size of a market.

Show your understanding

1. Calculate the value of business A's market share in 2009 and in 2011. Using your answers explain which you think should be most important to a business: market share or market growth?

2. Go back to Jamie's idea in the opening case study. Research the market size for the different smart-phone ecosystems. Which smartphone operating system (iOS, Blackberry, Android, Windows) has the highest market share? Which one has the highest market growth? Which operating system would you recommend Jamie to develop his application for? Explain your answer.

Market segmentation

Green and Black

In 2005, Cadbury bought Green and Black's. Why would it want to do this? The takeover price to Cadbury is unknown but thought to be around £20 million. Green and Black's existed to sell organic, dark chocolate products – hence the name. It started using Fairtrade cocoa in the early 1990s. As well as having a strong ethical stance, the business developed an enviable reputation for the flavour and quality of its products.

Cadbury had always thought of itself as an ethical business. In the nineteenth century it had pioneered employee-friendly practices. But its chocolate products were always designed for the mass market, conventional in style and quality. It would be hard to find a UK resident who has not eaten its products. Green and Black's appealed to a different, smaller, market, people who wanted high quality chocolate sourced in environmentally friendly ways and offering fair prices to cocoa growers. They were prepared to pay premium prices. This was a market segment that Cadbury could not easily reach with its existing products and its well-known image.

Questions

1. What impact would the acquisition of Green and Black's have on Cadbury's market share?

2. What other benefits might Cadbury get from owning the company?

Consumer groups

Personal tastes vary. They depend on individual preferences but they are also influenced by the kind of person you are. **Market segmentation** identifies different groups in society and studies their particular needs and wants.

Some products aim at a mass market – we all buy toothpaste. But even in that market, producers have identified a range of different needs. They produce differentiated products, e.g. toothpaste for sensitive teeth or with whitening qualities. A few products sell well in mass markets that run right across all sections of society – e.g. Coca Cola and unleaded petrol. But many markets for consumer products have segments that require different versions of the product to meet group needs precisely.

Products for segmented markets:	Markets segmented by:
Package holidays, e.g. cheap beach holidays, safaris, exotic locations	Age, income
TV stations, e.g. ITV1, BBC4, Yesterday	Age, education, hobbies
Housing – starter homes, flats, houses	Income, location, family size

> **Market segmentation** means that the market can be divided up into groups, each of which has distinctive customer preferences. Both products and marketing strategies can be differentiated to meet the requirements of each segment. Common groupings include age, gender, family status, income, interests, locations, culture, occupation, lifestyles etc.

Mass vs niche marketing

Mass marketing happens when a business aims a product at the largest part of the market. For example, Cadbury sell their Dairy Milk brand to the mass market by appealing to a very broad audience, often in different market segments.

Niche marketing means deliberately targeting a small group of customers, within a larger market, who all share the same characteristics or needs. Cadbury sell their organic, Fair Trade sourced Green and Black's brand chocolate to a niche market consisting of people who are concerned about environmental and ethical standards. Both niche and mass marketing can bring benefits as well as risks to the business.

Niche markets

	Mass marketing	Niche marketing
Benefits	• Large potential market could lead to large revenues	• Low levels of competition can lead to being able to charge a higher price, meaning increased revenue and profit • Clear focus – can target particular customers (who are often easier to find and reach)
Risks	• Strong competition can drive the price down, resulting in lower profits • Branding and advertising to large and diverse groups can be expensive and difficult	• Dependent on a small group of customers and vulnerable to changes in the market (all eggs in one basket) • Likely to attract competition if successful

Niche markets often develop around subcultures. For example, people who like world music form a very distinctive subculture which has its own festivals, recordings and friendship groups. Together they form a subculture. There are many other examples – people who like to go fishing, or enact historical battles, or get involved in amateur dramatics. Before you decide that these are all a bit weird, have a think about the subcultures you yourself value or have experienced.

> **Mass marketing** applies to a business that is aiming its product at the largest part of the market.
>
> **Niche marketing** means deliberately targeting a small group of customers, within a larger market, who share the same characteristics or needs

Show your understanding

Go back to Jamie's idea in the opening case study. Sketch images of typical customers for Jamie's smartphone app, identifying key segmentation information.

Is Jamie's smartphone app potentially a mass market or a niche market product? Explain your answer.

B&Q in China

Sales of DIY home improvement products topped £14bn in 2006. The market leader in this sector at this time was B&Q, which enjoyed around 24% market share, making their market share worth around £3.4bn.

B&Q executives were rightly proud of their company's performance in 2006. Their market share had increased from 19% in 1995 and the home improvement market had grown at an average rate of 7.8% for every year between 1997 and 2005, as customers were inspired by home improvement television shows like *Changing Rooms* and motivated by increasing property prices.

However, the boardroom was concerned that future company growth would be far harder to come by.

B&Q's increase in market share had been at the expense of Focus Do It All, Homebase and independent retailers but Wickes and a reinvigorated Homebase remained serious competitors in the retail sector whilst Travis Perkins was particularly strong in the wholesale sector. Significant increases in market share would be very expensive to achieve, requiring either costly takeovers, aggressive discounting or expensive marketing.

Furthermore, B&Q were concerned that the UK market would no longer continue to grow at such a rate. Changes in fashion were still expected but in terms of house decoration, the cycles of trend were far longer than those found in high street fashion.

By 2009 their fears were confirmed. The UK recession halted home improvement as disposable incomes fell and new housebuilding stopped almost entirely. The result was that the market shrank by around 15%. B&Q still enjoyed a healthy market share (still around 24%) but of a smaller market.

Nonetheless, B&Q executives were not overly worried because by 2005 they had opened altogether 48 B&Q branded stores in China. The Chinese home improvement market is estimated to be worth around £27bn; around twice as big as the UK's. Besides, growth in the Chinese home improvement market is around 15% per year.

The Water Saver

Having spent the summer in Africa volunteering, Lucy noticed how precious water is to African people. Inspired by this (and wondering if the West could carry on being so wasteful) Lucy designed a new shower-head that maintained a similar level of flow pressure whilst using 30% less water.

She tested her idea amongst her friends, using a prototype to verify that it worked before arranging for a manufacturer to take on production. As soon as she had a cost price (around £7) she approached B&Q with a view to stocking it in their stores. She worked out that the shower-head could save a family of four around £16 a year in water and demonstrated that it was easy to fit to existing showers. The B&Q product manager was impressed! Her positive reaction was confirmed when, later in the week, she called Lucy and agreed to stock the shower-head in the UK stores.

B&Q bought a number of Focus stores after the company went into administration in 2011, due to its recent losses.

Show your understanding

1. Calculate the value of the DIY home improvement market in 2009.

2. Calculate the value of B&Q's market share in 2009.

3. "B&Q's profits will have fallen in 2009." Discuss the accuracy of this statement.

4. Explain why B&Q needed to look abroad to achieve company growth.

5. Discuss whether Lucy should be worried about the recent negative market growth for DIY home improvement products.

6. Discuss whether Lucy should insist that her shower head be sold in Chinese branches of B&Q.

Find out

Visit http://neoformix.com/2011/UKAuto.png

What does the graphic show in terms of market size for *top ten cars*? Find out about the market for cars as a whole over the same time period.

Using the graphic, how could you segment the UK car market?

Chapter 9

Positioning the business idea

Are you nuts?

In the mid-1990s internet connections were slow; pages with pictures took a long time to load and social networking and streaming video were distant phenomena. Magazines were still the media for older teens and early twenties to explore fashion, music, celebrity, sport and adulthood. Monthly copies of *Just Seventeen, Bliss, More!* (sold fortnightly) and *Sugar* for girls and *FHM, Maxim* and *Loaded* for men sold well on the shelves of newsagents.

By the mid-2000s the internet had gathered pace and seriously threatened the sales of the magazines as their monthly publication cycle struggled to keep pace with rapidly changing trends. They offered readers very little opportunity to interact instantly with the magazine content. Faced with a dynamic market, magazine publishers needed to position new products to meet the changing needs of customers and compete with internet sites that could update content constantly.

It didn't take long for publishers to position several new magazines in the market. *Look!, Shout!* and *Heat* launched as weekly magazines aimed at young women whilst *More!* also moved to a weekly publication. For men *Nuts* and *Zoo* launched as weekly 'lad mags'. The move to weekly publication was a clear attempt to position the magazines much closer to readers' changing customer needs by providing a much more up to date view on fashion and celebrity. It also facilitated a much faster response to reader input through social media.

Discussion point

Explain why it was necessary for the magazine publishers to position their new businesses ideas as 'weekly' products.

Market positioning

In many markets, a range of similar products is available and each will have distinguishing features. (Think about the car industry.) Businesses like to have **differentiated products**. It helps them to cater for a range of market segments: they can design each product in the range so that it fits the requirements of a target segment quite precisely. These requirements can be discovered by doing careful market research and using the information obtained to make the product really attractive to customers. This is all part of market orientation – being sensitive to customer preferences. (See page 30.)

Market orientation

Another important aspect of product differentiation is that it helps the business to compete. A distinctive product, perhaps with a memorable brand name, will have particular attractions for many customers. But no matter how carefully designed the product is, if it is competing with a very similar product from another business, it will be much harder to sell in quantity.

This is where **market positioning** comes in. Most businesses look for a gap in the market – a group of potential customers whose needs are not well covered by existing products. This is what the publishers of *Nuts* and *Zoo* were doing. They positioned their magazines in a part of the market where there would be relatively little competition.

> **Differentiated products** are designed so that they have distinctive features that are different from those of competing products. The product may have unique characteristics or it may be marketed in a different way from its competitors, so that it has a distinct image.
>
> **Market positioning** refers to the way the product is perceived in comparison with competing products. Considering the positioning of the product helps the business to make decisions about the way its product range matches customer preferences or appeals to different market segments.

Market mapping

The best way to visualise the position of different products in the market is to use **market mapping**. There are two important aspects to consider when positioning a business idea.

● The business idea must be evaluated as to how well it will meet the customer needs that have been identified by market research. (See Chapters 7 and 8.) If it isn't going to meet current (or future) customer needs it is unlikely to be successful.

● Even if the product or service clearly meets the researched customer needs, it may be important that other businesses are not already doing that. Market mapping allows an entrepreneur to check whether this is the case.

Market maps

A market map sets out the features of the market on a diagram and then plots where each product fits in according to the market research findings. Each axis can represent a feature of the product or the market, or any possible way of segmenting the market. Each end of the axis is a polar opposite. These might include:

Feature	Segmentation
High quality vs lower quality	Male vs female
Mass vs niche market	Old vs young
Modern vs traditional	Urban customers vs rural customers
Aesthetic vs functional	High income customers vs low income customers
Luxury vs value	

Figure 9.1 shows what a market map for restaurants in a big city might look like. The features considered are price and atmosphere, which will be an important element in customer choice.

Figure 9.1 Which position?

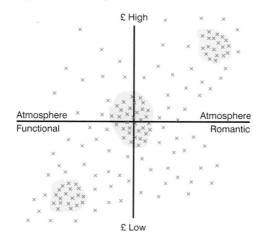

The market map below shows the UK 14-24 year old magazine market in the mid 2000s (for the case study on page 51). It uses a feature on the vertical axis and market segments – male vs female – on the horizontal axis.

Figure 9.2: The UK market for magazines for age 14-24, mid-2000s

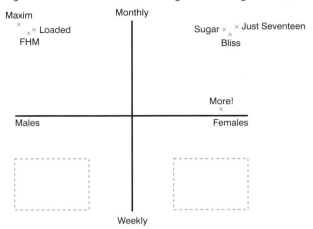

Finding a gap in the market

The three magazines in the top left corner of the map are positioned there because they are very focussed towards the male market. They are at the top of the map because they are all monthly magazines. *More!* is on the right hand side of the map because it meets the needs of females and is halfway between the top and the bottom of the map because it is fortnightly.

The market map allowed the publishers to check the level of potential competition and identify a **gap in the market**. There clearly were no products in the green areas for weekly magazines aimed at 14-24 year old males and females (either monthly, fortnightly or weekly). Positioning their products there would mean they would not face immediate competition.

Having used the market map to identify a gap and help position new products (e.g. *Nuts* and *Zoo*), the magazine publishers ultimately went ahead. They believed that customers had switched preferences, towards weekly magazines. However, the quote below is very useful for considering the main drawback with market mapping.

> *"There's a gap in the market but no market in the gap."* (Peter Jones, Dragons' Den).

Market mapping can highlight gaps in the market but the reality is that there can be a gap in the market for a good reason. It may be that no business has 'filled the gap' because there are few customers who want that combination of features from the product. Or maybe a previous business has tried and failed. This could be the case for a unisex magazine: trying to meet the needs of both segments could mean that the product would not fully meet the needs of either and therefore it would be unpopular.

 WATCH OUT!

There is often a gap in the market for luxury or high quality products at a low price. This may happen because businesses find it impossible to offer luxury or high quality at a low price; alternatively offering it at a low price may actually take the luxury feel away from the product.

Repositioning the product

Sometimes a product loses its attractions for its target market. If the business is making a loss on it, the best strategy may be to discontinue production. But sometimes it can be **repositioned** successfully. Lucozade did this; as a nutritional product for people in poor health, it was failing. Repackaged and advertised differently, it sold very well as an energy drink for fitness enthusiasts.

By 2012, some brands in the magazine market had repositioned themselves or left the market altogether. Publishers found that the *Sugar* brand no longer met its customer needs and it was discontinued, whilst the *Bliss* brand was repositioned to the 'tweenies' (ages 12-15) market.

A **market map** is a tool that plots brands in the market according to how they meet customers' needs. It allows a business to position individual products effectively.

A **gap in the market** indicates that there is scope for a new product that is not currently being provided.

Repositioning means targeting a different segment of the market, one where its individual features are more in keeping with the needs of the customer.

Show your understanding

1. Complete an up to date version of the market map for magazines in the UK, using your own choice of axes.

2. Do you think there are any current gaps in the market, creating an opportunity for a new magazine brand? If so, justify your thoughts.

3. Are there any brands that could do with repositioning? If so, justify your thoughts.

4. Explain why businesses sometimes reposition brands rather than creating new ones.

Evaluating the competition – strengths and weaknesses

Competing

The market mapping technique can illustrate areas where there are existing products attempting to meet customers' needs. Common sense would suggest that it would be wise to avoid this area of the market, especially if there is more than one competing product in that space.

However, it is entirely realistic for a new entrant into the market to deliberately position a new product in an area of the market map where there is already a brand. It will do this if it believes the competitor has a weakness. Or maybe it has strengths that can be overcome.

A product may have several weaknesses that would lead to a rival positioning their product in the same part of the market. These could include:
- high price
- low quality
- poor availability. This could include not being easily found by consumers in the places they expect, i.e. the lack of a convenient outlet or an online service
- slowness to respond to changing customer needs, perhaps due to outdated technology in the product or in production
- poor promotion leading to weak branding and brand loyalty.

Equally, however, an existing product may have some significant strengths that will put new competitors off from positioning their idea in a similar segment of the market. These could include:
- a loyal customer base
- if the business is large, it could temporarily reduce its price or engage in other promotional activities, in order to retain customers. This might last until the business with the new product gives up because it has been unable to compete on price or reputation
- customers may have long term contracts (as with mobile phone networks and health clubs), meaning that it is difficult for the new brand to gain customers quickly
- where the customer has already invested in the market. For example it will be hard to persuade people to swap to another manufacturer of digital cameras if they already have lots of lenses from a different brand that will be incompatible with the new brand.

SWOT

A new business will engage in a SWOT (Strengths, Weaknesses, Opportunities and Threats) analysis in order to evaluate their competitors before deciding where to position their brand. Essentially they will follow this process:

Show your understanding

1. Explain the purpose of market mapping.

2. Analyse why it is important to find a gap in the market.

3. Explain the steps a business could take to avoid a competitor positioning a new product or brand in a similar area of the market to itself.

4. Evaluate the extent to which product differentiation is necessary when entering a new market.

Competitive advantage

Once the competition has been evaluated, the new business (or the team developing the new product) can decide how it is going to gain **competitive advantage**. There are many ways of gaining a competitive edge which will help the business to succeed when competing with rivals. Price is important to competing successfully but **adding value** is also a key factor. All businesses do this to some extent, but the most successful will add more value.

Adding value

- Car manufacturers might design their brands to incorporate greater reliability.
- A beauty therapist might add value by getting some additional training, learning new ways of using beauty products effectively, or offering free styling advice.
- A theatre might add value by getting better known actors.

Adding value isn't costless but it can create a strong competitive advantage. It can make it possible to raise the price and still be perceived as offering good value for money.

Possible areas for gaining competitive advantage are shown in the diagram:

Competitive advantage may be achieved using any factor that will help the business to succeed when competing with rivals. Price may be important but there are many other ways of making a product competitive. Innovation, reputation and reliability can all be important.

Added value is the difference between the price that is charged and the total cost of the inputs needed to create the product. It applies to services as well as to manufactured goods. It may come from improving the product itself, or from improving the way markets perceive the product.

Competitive advantage

Show your understanding

For the following products or services, evaluate the relevance of each source of competitive advantage to their success:

- iPhone
- Netflix or LoveFilm
- Alton Towers
- Dyson vacuum cleaners

Fashion matters

Robyn graduated with a degree in Fashion design in 2010. Whilst studying and after she graduated she worked as a retail assistant at H&M, where she closely studied what customers like and their buying habits. Robyn now believes that with this experience in high street fashion retail and her knowledge of fashion design she is ready to set up her own fashion boutique.

The boutique will sell clothes designed by Robyn. She acknowledges that she will never achieve the low prices of the main high street brands, so will not be competing on price but does see the high street (Top Shop, River Island etc.) and online brands (ASOS.com etc.) as direct competition. She plans to gain competitive advantage by producing unique pieces to avoid what she describes as "the horror moment you get when you realise someone is wearing the same dress or shirt as you."

Robyn believes that she has found a gap in the market for a unisex shop, targeting customers aged between 17 and 28.

Questions

1. Describe how Robyn is planning to differentiate herself from the high street brands.

2. Explain two other methods that Robyn could use to gain competitive advantage.

3. Draw two market maps (with appropriate axes) to assist you in evaluating the extent to which Robyn has found a gap in the market, competing against the high street and online brands.

4. Discuss the usefulness of market mapping to Robyn as she attempts to position her brand.

Find out

Conduct some market research in a local town nearby and add any independent shops to the market map for fashion brands that you have drawn for Robyn. Would Robyn's store be positioned in a gap in the market in your town?

Chapter 10

What really works? Opportunity cost, test marketing and product trial

Taking decisions

Jim owned and ran a greengrocers shop in the High Street of a small town. Everyone said it was the best place for fruit and veg, anywhere in the town. Prices were quite high compared to the supermarket but the quality was excellent and Jim stocked everything you could possibly want. You could get all the things you needed for a new recipe and all the everyday greengroceries as well.

About two years after opening the shop, Jim rented the premises next door and knocked the walls down. That gave him a large open space to expand the greengrocery business and set up a small coffee area where customers could sit and eat delicious pastries or a light lunch. Sales revenue continued to climb.

After three more years, Jim found that he could make more money from the coffee shop than from the greengroceries. He saw that he had a choice. If he cut down the greengrocery space by half, he could put many more tables and chairs in for the coffee shop. That would increase the sales revenue from the coffee shop but might not make too much of a difference to the sales revenue from selling fruit and vegetables. He lay awake worrying about this. He just could not tell whether the gains from the one would be greater or less than the loss from the other.

In the end, Jim expanded the coffee shop and continued to sell fruit and vegetables from a smaller space. He stocked somewhat fewer items. He isn't saying how much his overall sales revenue increased but a few years later, he opened a second outlet in the big town ten miles away. The format was the same as his first outlet, so he must have made the right decision.

Questions
1. The greengrocery business was always successful. Why was Jim running a risk when he expanded the coffee shop?

2. How could Jim gather evidence that might help him to take the decision?

Choosing between alternatives

Jim's dilemma is a very familiar one. Every time we have a choice, we have to weigh up the pros and cons. We evaluate the alternatives. We have to do this because we never have enough resources to do everything we might want to do – resources are scarce, when compared to what we might want to do.

This means that every decision we make means going without some alternative.

● As a consumer you could be deciding between going to the cinema or buying a book like the one you are reading now, one that could be useful in helping you to understand your course on New Business Ideas.

● For Jim, the decision was between expanding one side of the business at the expense of the other. Many businesses have to decide whether to concentrate on existing products or launch new ones that may capture customers from a different market or market segment.

● For a government, the decision might be about spending more on military hardware. The alternative might be to spend more on welfare benefits for disabled people.

In each of these cases, the choice that is made will have an **opportunity cost**. That is what we are foregoing as a result of our choice. Jim was worried about foregoing some of his income from sales of greengroceries, when he expanded the coffee shop. You have taken a decision to study; the opportunity cost of studying is the income you might be earning if you can work. Governments are worrying all the time about spending priorities and the opportunity cost of their expenditures.

Trade-offs

Opportunity cost

Where there is a choice, there is an opportunity cost. Having one thing, or following one course of action, means not having something else. Choosing between the cinema ticket and the text book is like this. But often, the choice is rather different – it is between more of A and less of B, or more of B and less of A. This definitely applied to Jim's decision – he was never going to shut down either side of his business. This means there is a **trade-off** between one choice and the other, or others.

> The **opportunity cost** of a decision is the value which is expected to flow from the next best alternative decision. When making a choice between possible alternatives, the opportunity cost of any spending decision is made clear.
>
> **Trade-offs** occur when two things cannot be fully achieved. Having more of one thing may mean having less of the other.

Style vs. price

Tata

Tata is a huge Indian conglomerate, a business that makes many different products. It owns JLR (Jaguar Land Rover) as well as much of the UK steel industry. In 2010 it launched the Nano car, designed specifically for the Indian market. To sell well there, the price had to be low – it started at around £1750. Obviously it is basic compared to cars sold in western markets, but it is affordable in India, at least for some people.

Many people, including the Tata management, thought the Nano would sweep the market. In the event, sales were disappointing. No one wanted to buy the world's cheapest car. In the post mortem some commentators said that Tata had made some bad decisions:

- The advertising emphasised the low price. Some said Tata had put too much effort into cost savings and not enough into sex appeal.

- Others said that the senior managers at Tata had taken their eyes off the ball. They were so excited about taking over JLR that they put all their energy into making that work, and overlooked the need to monitor the development of the Nano.

- Better market research could have alerted the Tata management to the difficulties it would face in the market. More emphasis might have been put on the efficiency of the air conditioning (an important factor in India), or other product features.

Questions

1. What was the opportunity cost of focusing solely on keeping the price of the Nano down to the absolute minimum?

2. What evidence is there that Tata faced a trade-off between getting the Nano right and ensuring that the takeover of JLR was a success?

Could Tata have known in advance that the decision to take over Jaguar Land Rover would make it difficult to give full attention to promoting the Nano? Perhaps in the long run both ventures will prove to be a success. At the time of writing, sales of the Nano are picking up, especially to women and people living in

What do you think?

the smaller Indian cities. Demand for JLR vehicles is so high that they are expanding capacity and taking on more employees at their UK factories.

Very often, businesses have to decide between developing one product rather than another. In business and in everyday life, every decision involves weighing up two (or possibly more) alternatives. Almost always, a decision to do one thing means foregoing something else.

Test marketing

Taking decisions in business is difficult. Often they have to be taken using incomplete information. Estimates may be somewhat different from the reality as it turns out. One way to reduce the risks of launching a new product is to try it out by **test marketing** in a limited area. In this way, it may be possible to find out whether the product will be profitable. It creates an opportunity to see how the product sells without risking the huge investment required to set up full-scale production of the new product.

Reducing risks

Should Tata have test marketed the Nano, trying it out, say in just one Indian province? Would this have revealed design shortcomings, which could have been rectified before the main product launch? This approach would probably have been far too expensive for a complex product like a car. But it is much more feasible with everyday consumer products, and it can work well for food products .

New products will be tried out on focus groups, with people who volunteer to taste the product and comment on it. If they approve of the flavour, texture and so on, the product will then be launched on a small scale in a particular area.

> **Test marketing** means that the new product will be marketed and sold within a small area to see how potential customers react to it. This market needs to have similar features to the ultimate target market. It is quite an expensive way to discover whether the product will sell, but it may be a lot cheaper than a full-scale launch of a product for which there is little demand.

Test marketing

Island Analyses

This is a company that organises test marketing on the islands of Jersey, Guernsey or the Isle of Man. The idea is that these islands are isolated from the rest of the UK and advertising within the islands will be easier, cheaper and more efficient than on the mainland. Also, in Guernsey in particular, the age, social and occupational structures of the population closely resemble those of the UK market as a whole. So test marketing done there is likely to provide conclusions that would apply to the wider market.

Island Analyses reckons these factors mean that it can offer reasonably priced services that will give valuable information about the likely impact of the new product in the wider market.

Show your understanding

1. Why would food products be particularly suitable for test marketing?

2. What other kinds of products might be suitable for test marketing?

3. What disadvantages does test marketing have?

Test marketing can be used before production begins, sometimes even before the product development stage is complete. The idea is that both the product and the marketing strategy can be evaluated by small groups of customers, in the context of a normal retailing situation and without the customers realising that this is happening. You may have been in a department store or supermarket where someone is standing by a table with delicate nibbles or drinks, inviting you to help yourself and comment on the product you have been offered. At the end of the day conclusions will be drawn on the customer reaction to the product. The conclusions may be used to adapt the product to make it more attractive.

Product trial

Test marketing is just one way of achieving **product trial** – making sure that people actually try the unfamiliar product to see if they like it. If they do, then the possibility of **repeat purchases** will greatly increase the chances of the product's succeeding.

Getting consumers to try a new product can be difficult, especially if it is competing with many popular existing products. Often in the launch phase, large sums of money will be spent on advertising to make people aware of the new product's existence. But if the advertising suggests that the product is truly wonderful, and it turns out to be just another version of an existing product, the advertising may backfire. This will mean disappointing levels of repeat purchase.

Repeat purchases

Product trial refers to the way customers will buy something once to see if they like it.

Repeat purchases occur when the customer decides to buy the product on a regular basis.

Sometimes new products start out being quite expensive. If they are really innovative and attractive as well, they will face little competition and the business can charge a high price and still sell the product. But when potential competing businesses see the success of the product, they will come along with me-too versions. This happened with bagless vacuum cleaners and liquid laundry detergents.

To ensure that a new product gets repeat purchases, it has to be highly competitive. It must:
- be something people do want
- offer good value for money, in terms of quality if not price
- be marketed in ways that ensure widespread recognition
- be displayed where people will notice it.

Yorkie

The chocolate bar that came out in 1975 and is still selling well must be a good example of a repeat purchase. It is worth looking at the development process it went through. It was Rowntree's answer to Cadbury's Dairy Milk (selling since 1905).

Cadbury had reduced the thickness of the Dairy Milk bar, because of rising sugar and cocoa prices. Market research showed that customers did not like this. Rowntree set to work to find an answer to a range of consumer needs that the research had identified and produced edible samples, packaging and advertising material for four new products:
- a chocolate bar with nuts and port wine flavour and advertising associations from the 1900s
- a thick bar with countryside associations
- a box of milk chocolate pieces and a continental image
- a chunky milk chocolate bar with masculine associations, called 'Rations'.

More market research followed; all four concepts were tested on four groups of consumers. They liked the last one, but not the name, which was changed to Yorkie, possibly because it was to be made in York.

Questions

1. Explain why a focus group was an appropriate way to review the four proposed products.
2. How would you explain the success of the Yorkie bar?

Find out

Over the next three weeks, look out for new products in adverts, on display, in the news or come across by word of mouth. What makes you think that the product might or might not succeed? Compare your findings with those of others in your group.

Stakeholders

Impact on people

Wherever there are decisions to be made, there will be trade-offs and the interests of different groups of people will be affected. Each decision will impact upon a stakeholder group in a different way. Stakeholders include all those people who are directly affected by business decisions.

Stakeholder groups include customers, employees, shareholders, suppliers and the wider community, all of which are affected by the actions of the business.

The effects of decisions on stakeholders can be seen in many everyday situations.

- When Honda decided to expand its car factory in Swindon, the employees and the local community were cheered by the offer of more jobs.

- A new product that turns out to be unprofitable usually means that some customers have been disappointed, and the shareholders might be too.

- A business that strives to improve efficiency and makes some employees redundant, but makes a bigger profit in consequence, will please the shareholders but anger the employees.

Think

Which stakeholders will feel the impact, and how, if the business improves customer service?

Chapter 11

Looking at the economy

Two businesses – different stories

Travel agents have had a tough time. Competition from direct on-line booking has reduced their profits over a long period. On top of that, recession conditions and falling or very slow growing incomes mean some people are cutting back on holidays abroad. Thomas Cook, one of the UK's oldest travel businesses, made a fairly modest loss of £269 million in the first half of 2011 but that rose in 2012 to £713 million. The business operates worldwide but even so, that is a very serious loss.

Jaguar Land Rover, on the other hand, was doing well in 2012. Tata Motors, its Indian parent company, announced that it would raise spending on new products from an annual £1.5 billion to £2 billion. It planned to replace its Range Rover top-of-the-range model and build a new engine plant in Wolverhampton. Sales in China had increased by 75% over the previous year and the company planned to increase the level of shift working in its UK factories. After-tax profits doubled.

Both these businesses were operating against a background of generally difficult trading conditions in the UK economy as a whole.

Questions

1. List three possible reasons why Thomas Cook was in difficulty.

2. How might the business deal with the rising losses? Outline two possibilities.

3. Why were things rather different at JLR?

The economic cycle

The national economy

The business environment is quite dynamic. Things are always happening – demand changes, costs and prices change. Governments change too – and not just at election time. New policies may be introduced. Change is normal. Businesses have to keep a sharp eye on the changes that might affect them and adapt as fast as they can.

Figure 11.1: Real GDP growth, annual % change

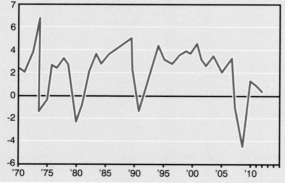

Source: ONS; NB 'Real' means that inflation has been allowed for; 2012 = estimate

One key question recurs, is the economy growing and by how much? In general a growing economy means growing demand for many businesses. A few businesses do better when the economy isn't growing (remember Domino's in Chapter 6?) Either way entrepreneurs need to know what is going on, and be aware of the **economic cycle**.

Figure 11.1 shows how and when **Gross Domestic Product** (**GDP**) has grown (or not) since 1970.

- Why so long ago? Because the graph shows how the economy fluctuates, in cycles.

- Why GDP? This just means the sum total of all production in the economy. The statisticians add up all the output, all the income and all the spending – which are three different ways of measuring the same thing. The percentage change in GDP is a measure of **economic growth**.

These cycles are referred to in three ways – but they all mean the same thing. The business cycle, the economic cycle and the trade cycle are just different ways of describing the fluctuations. Here we are using the term economic cycle, but if you get asked about the business cycle in an exam, remember, the two are no different.

The economic cycle

The **economic cycle** is the sequence of depression, recovery, boom and recession which creates significant fluctuations in demand for many products. Also known as the business cycle or the trade cycle.

Gross domestic product (**GDP**) is a measure of the size of the economy and gives the money value of all output. It is also used as a measure of national income and total expenditure in the economy. GDP or incomes in real terms refer to data that has had the effects of inflation removed.

Economic growth means an increase in the total output of the economy. If it is rising, the standard of living should improve. Many businesses will experience rising demand for their products.

Booms and recessions

Looking at Figure 11.1, you can see that most of the time the, the economy is growing by between 2% and 4% each year. This is a happy story – most years, for most people, there has been a little more income to spend or save. Standards of living have risen. But every so often – in 1974, 1980, 1989 and 2008 – there has been an abrupt change in which economic growth slowed and went below zero, i.e. negative, so that the economy actually shrank. Those downturns were recessions – output fell but only for a short time. If output falls for longer, there is a depression – as happened in the 1930s. To see what the phases of the economic cycle are actually like, look at the table.

	Depression	Recovery	Boom	Recession
Unemployment	High	High but falling	Low	Rising
Inflation	Low	Stable	Accelerating	Falling
Confidence	Very low	Rising	High	Falling
Investment	Very little	Growing slowly	Growing faster	Falling

Causes of recession

Recessions usually have more than one cause. In 1974 and 1980, huge oil price rises were very much part of the story. When people and businesses have to pay much more for petrol, they are left with less money to spend on other things, so many businesses find it harder to sell their products. In 1989 and 2008 the economy had been allowed to expand fast and in an unsustainable way. In keeping cyclical movements to a minimum, government policies can help or hinder. But economies do have a tendency to expand and contract all on their own. Figure 11.2 shows the phases of the economic cycle and the long term trend rate of economic growth as standards of living gradually rise.

The economic cycle plays a big part in determining the levels of unemployment and inflation. This will become clearer later.

Figure 11.2: The economic cycle

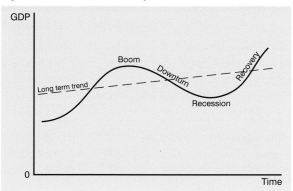

What was wrong in 2012?

Current trends

Well, quite a lot. In 2007-08, the credit crunch, a banking crisis in which the banks all lost confidence, meant that they stopped lending to each other. This caused a fall in spending generally because loans became very hard to get. The economy was in any case sliding slowly towards recession. Business confidence took a big hit: few businesses wanted to invest significantly in new production facilities. So spending fell further. As unemployment rose, many people found their incomes falling and so spent less. The economy got into a vicious downward spiral.

Find out

By the time you read this, the economy will have moved on. Find out what has happened since 2012 to GDP, inflation and unemployment. How would you describe the current level of business confidence? Have you come across businesses that are planning to invest and expand? Do you know why they believe they could succeed?

The banking crisis led to fewer loans, less spending and greater unemployment.

Unemployment

The data

Figure 11.3: Unemployment, 2008-2012

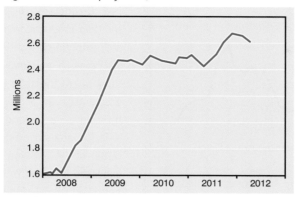

Source: ONS

Figure 11.4: Part-time working

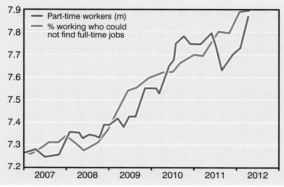

Source: ONS

Figure 11.5: Average earnings

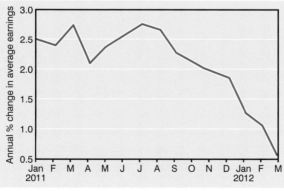

Source: ONS

Between 2000 and 2008, the number of unemployed people hovered between 1.5 and 1.7 million, mostly about 5.5% of the labour force, which was more than most people would want but not too serious. Figure 11.3 shows how unemployment rocketed in 2008-9. Actually it could have been worse. Many employers tried to avoid making people redundant and kept on as many people as they could. They offered shorter hours or part-time work and some people accepted a pay cut rather than lose their jobs (see Figures 11.4 and 11.5). This meant that employers could be ready and able to expand as soon as demand improved.

⚠ WATCH OUT!

The axes do not start at zero. Remember to look for this when you are trying to interpret the data.

Remember that if earnings increase by less than the rate of inflation, *real* incomes are falling.

Recession continued

Unfortunately, in 2012, although there had been short periods of relative buoyancy in the economy, the turnaround had not yet begun. This story is very typical of recession conditions. 2.6 million is about 8.2% of the work force. In addition, there may be many people who would like to work but do not qualify for unemployment benefits and have given up looking.

The smaller increase in unemployment, in 2011, suggested the start of what is called a double-dip recession. A possible reason for this could be the painful expenditure cuts, which governments all over Europe were using as a way of reducing their large deficits. The difficulty is that in a recession, part of the large deficit comes from paying increased unemployment benefits while receiving less in tax revenue because incomes for many people are falling. There is more in this in Chapter 12.

Inlation

Figure 11.6: Inflation

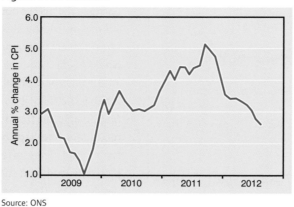

Source: ONS

In a booming economy, demand is growing fast. Businesses can put up prices and still sell their products. In a recession, businesses are competing in a shrinking market and they will be much more inclined to keep prices the same or cut them. So inflation automatically accelerates in a boom and slows in a recession. For a long period up to 2007, inflation rates stayed close to the government target of 2% and you might therefore have expected inflation to fall below that in the period 2008-12. Figure 11.6 shows what actually happened.

Unemployment occurs when there are people who want to work but cannot find a job. High unemployment is wasteful: resources, in the form of people, are not producing anything and the government has to increase the amount spent on unemployment benefits.

Inflation is a sustained rise in the general level of prices for goods and services. If incomes stay the same, purchasing power will fall. Inflation can be measured in different ways. The Consumer Price Index (CPI) is used when comparing inflation rates internationally. The Retail Price Index (RPI) is used as a basis for setting pay and pensions.

Rising prices

The economic cycle is not the only influence on inflation. Rising commodity prices are a big factor. When oil prices rise, petrol and energy bills go up fast and have a big impact. Prices of minerals like copper and some food prices may also rise (or fall). Prices go up when VAT rises. When inflation rose in the period 2009-11, all of these figured amongst the suggested causes. To explain this, we have to take a look at global trends.

Inflation causes problems for businesses because it makes the future more uncertain. It is harder to estimate likely future demand for the product and to take decisions about possible expansion. It also creates uncertainty for individuals, who may feel less clear about their likely future standard of living.

Globalisation

Over the past twenty years, there has been a big increase in international trade. Cheap imports of manufactured products have raised standards of living because people have been able to buy more with the amount they could earn. Export opportunities have increased too. World markets have become increasingly integrated. This means that countries that trade with one another become interdependent. They depend on one another for supplies of the products they want and for markets for the products they produce.

Globalisation also means that individual economies become more vulnerable to events elsewhere. Wars and civil disturbances can disrupt supplies of oil but can also mean that a previously useful market for other countries' exports is closed off. Falling demand in the economy of a trading partner, for any reason, can be very bad for exporters.

Globalisation refers to the way in which all the world's economies have become more closely integrated. There is more trade in products and services. There is foreign investment and many businesses are active in more than one country.

The impact of exchange rates

Understanding the UK economy is impossible without including the exchange rate in the story. Figure 11.7 shows that the pound fell by a total of 25% between 2006 and the end of 2008. This meant that if nothing else changed:

Imports and exports

- Imports would be 25% dearer in late 2008 than they had been in 2006. `

- Exports would be 25% cheaper in foreign markets. Foreign buyers would find UK products much more competitive than before.

- It would be far easier to compete in 2009-10 than it had been in 2006. Exporters would be able to sell more in foreign markets and UK businesses would find it easier to compete with imports.

Figure 11.7: The UK exchange rate

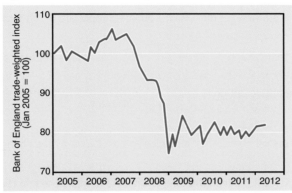

Source: Bank of England

Of course, it takes businesses and consumers a little while to adapt to new exchange rates. But Figure 11.8 shows that in the two years after the dramatic fall in the UK exchange rate, exports rose by 20%. However, imports really did not change very much. All that can be said is that they rose by a bit less than exports.

Figure 11.8: Export and import volumes

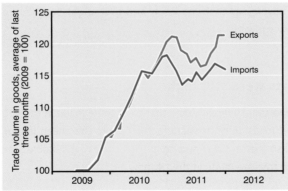

Source: ONS

An **exchange rate** is the rate at which one currency is exchanged for another. Usually exchange rates change continuously, but by small amounts. An economy that is struggling to compete is likely to find its exchange rate falling.

**Competitive-
ness**

> ## ⚠ WATCH OUT!
>
> Figure 11.7 uses the exchange rate index to measure the change in the currencies of the UK's main trading partners as a group. The value of 100 was given for the base year, 2009, so it is easy to see the percentage change. You do not need a deep understanding of this process but you must be able to interpret the figures correctly, i.e. spot the percentage change.

Evidence

1. Some businesses are expanding – JLR are one example but other car companies like Honda in Swindon have announced big new investments. UK-produced vehicles are selling well because they are cheaper than imported competitors. But this is probably not the major factor for JLR – they are benefiting from the huge increase in demand for luxury products in China. They have, quite simply, found a big new market. Rich Chinese people are often more concerned with status, quality and branding than with price.

2. Some manufacturers that have been getting their products made in China are rethinking their strategies. The change in the exchange rate, together with big pay increases in China, have made this a rather less competitive option.

Discussion points

(a) To what extent can the car companies' new plans be explained by the change in the exchange rate?

(b) Why might it make sense for a manufacturer of trainers to make them in the UK instead of an emerging economy like China?

(c) Discuss whether or not consumers in the UK might buy more UK-made clothes if they were 25% cheaper.

(d) 'Drink up' is a small independent retailer selling interesting but inexpensive wines. It sells locally as well as online. How will the owners of the business feel about a fall in the pound? What consequences will it have?

(e) Think of two small businesses that you know and that might be affected by exchange rate changes. Explain how and why.

Explaining why imports were still high

● Globalisation involved importing some products that used to be made in the UK. If cheap labour made it possible to cut prices, it made sense to manufacture where the cheap labour was. Because of this, some UK factories closed so that in time, no one at all was making suitable substitute products in the UK. For example, very few toys are made in the UK now.

● Some UK businesses, like Burberry, were still making substitutes for imports, but designing them to sell as luxury items, with prices *more* than 25% above the old import prices.

● Using the example of the trainer manufacturer above, it might take some time to organise all the production facilities they would need if they were to relocate their manufacturing operations back to the UK.

● Many UK exports require imported inputs – components, or raw materials. When exports rise, some imports will rise too.

High imports meant that many UK businesses were still having difficulty competing with products from abroad. Holidays in the UK were still often expensive and risky in terms of weather.

At the time of writing, the eurozone crisis and austerity policies generally (designed to cut government deficits) are leading to weak demand. This makes it very hard to sell exports to the countries concerned (see the case study below). More than half the UK's exports go to the EU. So exports are not as high as might have been expected.

The exchange rate and inflation

Import prices

When import prices rise, inflation rises. Many of the products we buy are imported, so if we are measuring inflation, we have to include imports. Some of the inflation mentioned above can be blamed on the fall in the exchange rate. When the Bank of England needs to explain to the public why inflation has been quite high, this is given as an important reason. A lower exchange rate means you have to pay more for what you import.

Imports are not just things brought to us by sea or by air. They include many services. The vast numbers of tourists who come to London are buying UK exports. When we holiday abroad we are buying imports.

If rates of pay are rising, costs will rise and products will cost more. This will push up the rate of inflation, but it will also make the economy concerned less competitive.

Show your understanding

You are about to go on holiday in France and have £100 spending money to exchange for euros. If the euro goes down against the pound, how will this affect your spending power?

Would an exporter of scotch whisky want the pound to be high or low? Say why.

Postscript – Greece and the euro

One reason for the low level of business confidence in 2012 was the eurozone crisis. The Greek government's borrowing had reached levels at which lenders felt very doubtful that it would ever be possible for them to be paid back. Greece had a huge external deficit (imports far exceeded exports) because many businesses had gradually lost competitiveness within the eurozone. So Greece could not sell enough exports to pay for its imports. Loss of export markets meant falling demand for Greek products. So incomes were falling, tax revenue was falling and the bill for unemployment benefit was rising. There was a plan to rescue Greece, largely with money from Germany. But there were very strict conditions attached to this bail out – involving huge cuts in government spending. The Greek voters decided to reject these austerity conditions and the German voters said OK, no bail-out.

Next?

In this kind of situation, a fall in the exchange rate can restore competitiveness. The effect on the standard of living is tough; however a few years hard work can put the economy back on its feet. But Greece was a small country in the eurozone. The euro wasn't going to fall just because of Greece – It was held up by the strength of other member economies.

Question

What happened next? If you don't know, find out.

Chapter 12

How does economic change affect people and businesses?

Reducing the deficit

When the coalition government came to power in 2010, it was perfectly clear that the government would need to economise. Even the Labour opposition said that they would have to cut spending. Government spending had exceeded tax revenue for some time. It was obvious that the financial institutions that lend to the UK government were becoming less confident and would require progressively higher rates of interest in the future. George Osborne, Chancellor of the Exchequer, wanted to restore confidence in the UK government and to do that, he planned to cut spending and raise taxes. He promised to eliminate the deficit by 2015 – the expected date of the next election.

The Chancellor succeeded in restoring confidence. Soon the UK government was able to borrow at far lower rates of interest than most other governments. But the deficit remained stubbornly high. In the 2012 Budget, Mr Osborne announced new investment projects, designed to improve the UK's infrastructure by building and improving roads and bridges, as well as other vital facilities that could in the long run make businesses more productive.

Discussion points

(a) One of the road improvements was a notorious bottleneck on the A21 in Kent, that was holding up traffic even with the economy in recession. What type of business might benefit from this kind of development, and how?

(b) Mr Osborne cut spending on defence and certain disability benefits, among many other things. Consider in each case how these cuts would affect the economy. (Example: cuts in grants to local authorities could reduce their spending on parks and gardens. This is likely to mean that some of the gardeners lose their jobs. Those people will have lower incomes if they cannot find other jobs. They will spend less and this will result in lower levels of demand for some consumer products. Some businesses will find their sales revenue falling and if they are near the edge, they may end in closing down, leading to further job losses.)

Government expenditure and tax revenue

Public spending

Over the long run, governments in the UK usually account for very roughly 40% of economic activity. The government has its own employees – civil servants, the staff in local council offices, NHS employees (over 1 million of them), teachers, the armed forces and so on. This is what we call the **public sector**. But the government also pays many businesses to carry out the services it requires. Veolia is a big company specialising in recycling and waste management generally and works for many local authorities, which pay **private sector** businesses to do the jobs that need doing.

For some big businesses, the government is the customer. Small businesses do not get many opportunities in this field. Getting a government contract usually means getting into a tender process, which means bidding for the job. This in itself requires particular skills and the backing of an organisation. Government agencies do use consultants, who may be individuals with their own small business, to do certain kinds of work e.g. running small scale training projects. But for the most part, suppliers of government services are big.

So government expenditure pays for many jobs in both the public and private sector. When the government cuts expenditure, almost always there will be job cuts. Many people who are made redundant will not find it easy to get another job quickly. Their income will fall, probably for a time to the level of any benefits they can get. They will spend less and many businesses will face falling sales revenue. Small businesses are more likely to be hit hard, because they have limited savings from past profits. So they are the ones least likely to survive a period of slack demand. Closing businesses means even more redundancies and the process can continue in a vicious circle. Everyone will feel less confident about the future.

> **Government expenditure:** spending by the government on services to the public, e.g law and order, welfare benefits for the elderly, disabled and unemployed, public housing etc. Decisions are likely to be taken in the public interest, rather than for profit.
>
> **Public sector:** that part of the economy that is directly organised by the government, either local or national, using its own employees.
>
> **Private sector:** all the businesses and self-employed people that take their decisions independently. They must at least cover their costs if they are to stay alive, and most will see making a profit as an important objective.

There is a third sector that is growing gradually, over the years – the voluntary sector. In includes charities, not-for-profit and community organisations. This is like the private sector in that organisations that cannot cover their costs will not survive for long. It includes hospices, clubs, professional associations and a host of other small ventures run by groups of committed people.

Expenditure cuts

Wherever there is government spending, cuts will have a direct effect on employment and incomes. The flow chart shows how this plays out. Sometimes the *threat* of redundancies is enough to make people spend less – loss of confidence makes both employees and employers cautious. Equally, if the economy starts to grow again and confidence returns, a virtuous circle will follow in which there will be money to expand both public and private sector activity and incomes and employment will rise.

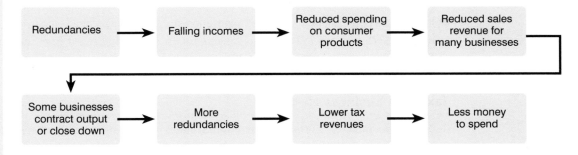

Paying for public services

Taxing and borrowing

Tax revenue is vital to pay for services. When unemployment is low and incomes are growing, tax revenue will be growing too. More services look affordable. For a long period, from the mid 1990s until 2007, it seemed that the economy was growing in a sustainable way, incomes rose and tax revenues rose. Both governments and individuals could spend more. Some of that time, the government spent less than it received in tax revenue – there was a surplus. Later it borrowed more.

Borrowing can fund investments in new projects and expansion of public services such as the NHS. When the economy grows more slowly and recession is looming any past surplus and borrowing can together make it possible to keep employment and incomes from falling. The government stimulates the economy with more spending. If this works fairly quickly to get the economy going everyone benefits –

businesses can stay in business and most employees keep their jobs. (This is not what happened in the period 2008-12.)

When taxes are increased to pay for higher spending, the economy changes but does not actually shrink. But if taxes are increased to reduce the government deficit, everyone has less spending power and we get the kind of outcome shown in the flow chart above.

Spending more on community care

As fewer and fewer people stay in hospital for a long time, care in the community has expanded. Governments are spending more on community care, partly to keep NHS costs down and partly to care better for the ageing population. Much of this community care is actually provided by small businesses. They usually call themselves care agencies and they can be not-for-profit organisations but many are, quite simply, businesses.

Money spent on community care comes partly from tax revenue. Expenditure cuts in this area will reduce the agencies' revenue and profits.

Discussion point

How would falling revenue affect a care agency? What would actually happen if demand decreases?

Some changes have helped business

Corporation tax

● Taxes are levied on businesses as well as people. Corporation tax in 2012 took 20% of profit for businesses with turnover up to £300,000 per year. Up to 2010, the rate was 21%. Obviously this will help small businesses – a bit. Bigger businesses pay a little more in corporation tax, the rate rising to 24% where turnover is above £1.5 million. The rate in 2010 was 28%, and in 2013 it goes down to 23%. This is a much more substantial cut but it will not help small businesses except insofar as they may get more orders from growing customer businesses. Neither cut will help businesses that are making no profit at all.

● In 2012 the Department for Business, Innovation and Skills (BIS) offered employers a wage incentive of up to £2,275 for each job they could create for an 18 to 24 year-old from the Government's Work Programme, if the job lasted at least 26 weeks.

Tax – the business view

Besides corporation tax, businesses pay Business Rates – to their local authorities. These can be a hefty expense and add to their costs. Essentially business rates are just another tax. Arguably they pay for the services that businesses require, but not everyone sees it that way.

South Road

In 2011, many of the shop owners and cafés in the street got angry about their business rates. Almost all are small businesses, with just the one outlet. Sonia's World of Cakes specialises in cakes for celebrations – their adverts say 'Our only limit is your imagination'. They had to pay £4,850 to Sefton Council. This is enough to make a big dent in profits. Sonia said "The amount of money we have to pay in business rates is not fair."

VAT

For a very long time Value Added Tax (VAT) stood at 17.5%. It is paid on sales of all consumer products except for food eaten at home, housing, books and newspapers and public transport (with a few other exceptions). In late 2008 it was reduced to 15%, to give people a bit more spending power and lift the

Taken in Euston Road, London NW1, soon after Budget Day, 2009.

economy generally. In January 2010 it went back up to 17.5%. When VAT rises, most retailers put the price up to cover the extra tax. But not quite all do. Just a few will hold the price to keep the competition away. (As of 2012, VAT was 20%.) The same applies to other sales taxes, like alcohol duty.

The main problem with VAT from the business point of view is that an increase puts up prices and reduces customers' spending power. If the product is something customers can manage without, sales revenue will fall. VAT also creates an administrative burden. In general business communities usually favour tax cuts and dislike tax increases because of the effect on demand across the economy.

Monetary policy

Interest rates

The Bank of England tries to keep inflation under control, mainly by adjusting interest rates. When the Bank of England changes its interest rate, all the banks adjust their lending rates by a similar percentage. If the rate goes up, business loans become more expensive, along with mortgages and personal loans. It gets harder for businesses to expand and for consumers to buy homes and big ticket items like cars. It is also harder for businesses to raise prices and this slows down the rate of inflation.

In 2006-2008, inflation was inching upwards and the Bank of England kept its interest rate around 5%. But as the recession deepened, the economy needed a stimulus and the rate was cut. Since early 2009, it has been at kept at 0.5%, phenomenally low. The idea was to encourage spending at a time when demand in the economy was at a very low level.

The snag was that confidence was so low in the period 2008-12 that few businesses dared to expand. Many didn't want loans at any price. Similarly, mortgages were so hard to get that the price to be paid for them – the interest rate – hardly mattered. However, the low rate clearly did have some value:

● Homeowners with mortgages found their monthly payments were reduced and this gave them a bit more spending power.

● When demand does rise, the low rate will help new businesses, for as long as it lasts.

● Small businesses that could find a market and could get a loan did get started.

**Competitive-
ness**

Show your understanding

Pete Reynolds lost his job as a department manager in a DIY store that closed down in 2009. He decided to try garden maintenance and targeted the growing number of elderly people who find the bigger garden jobs more than they can manage. Peter had to buy a van, a mower and hedge cutting gear and he needed insurance – some gardening jobs can lead to accident or injury. He got a small bank loan and his income, though less than previously, was just enough to live on.

Other people were not so lucky because although bank loans were cheap, they were very hard to get. Banks were very wary. They had taken too many risks in the past and changed their approach. So many people with good ideas found either that the process of getting a loan was very long and slow, or that the bank refused to lend anything at all.

Question

Peter's solution sounds easy enough. Explain three reasons why most redundant employees do not go along a similar route.

The impact of exchange rate changes

Chapter 11 showed how a low exchange rate favours exporters and UK businesses that compete with imports. A low rate makes both groups more competitive. But there are other businesses and people for whom a low exchange rate is not so helpful.

- When the exchange rate falls, the price of imported inputs rises. This raises costs of production. This can affect all sorts of products from tinned sardines to electrical goods and some UK businesses will raise their prices, making them less competitive.

- Retailers, including the supermarkets, that sell imported products, will also suffer when they have to pay more for their imported stock. They will have to choose between putting the price up, which means losing some sales, and keeping it the same and losing some profit.

- Some people may benefit from a lower exchange rate, especially if they can get a job in a business that exports. But most people will find that the rising prices of imports mean their purchasing power is reduced. For example, holidays abroad will cost more. They will simply have to buy less and their standards of living may fall.

Think!

Would you be a gainer or a loser if the £ fell further this year? Remember, the effects of the fall in the exchange rate will take 2-3 years to work through completely.

Inflation has consequences – pros and cons

A business with big bank loans may find that when it is time to pay back the loan, its value *in terms of its purchasing power* is actually less. This could be helpful. But the other likely consequences of inflation are much less so:

- Inflation can mean losing competitiveness. This happened in the UK in the 1970s. It happened in Greece in recent years. Exports will be hard to sell and imports selling all too easily. The problem can be avoided if the exchange rate is free to fall, but that reduces stability.

- Inflation is unpredictable – this uncertainty makes it harder for businesses to plan for the future.

- There are accounting issues. Sales revenue may rise just because prices rose – but this disguises the fact that the business really did not grow. Accounts need to be interpreted with care.
- Businesses with fixed price contracts may find profits falling if their costs rise.

The labour market

Trouble at the tank factory

In 2012, BAe Systems decided to close its Armstrong Plant in Newcastle upon Tyne. 620 jobs were at stake. The factory produced the Terrier engineering vehicle, which builds trenches and barriers. But government expenditure cuts, and the drawing to a close of the war in Afghanistan, meant that no more government orders could be expected. It was a sad time for local people – during the First World War the factory had produced tanks and ships and had long traditions.

For the many skilled people amongst the workforce, there was hope. Nissan, with the largest UK car manufacturing plant nearby in Sunderland, was known to be hiring. It would look out for people with scarce skills.

Questions

1. Would there be any point in trying to keep the Armstrong Plant open?
2. What would be the likely impact of the closure on small businesses nearby and in the north east generally?
3. How would these small businesses react?
4. How might Nissan benefit from the closure?

Recruiting

A tight labour market goes along with high levels of demand and boom conditions. To recruit, employers will have to offer higher pay. But when there is a high level of unemployment, the pressure for pay rises may be much less. Pay seldom falls, but it may stay the same for many employees for some time, whatever the rate of inflation. This means that purchasing power falls – very much a feature of life in the period 2008-12, when many people got pay rises that were less than the rate of inflation. In general:

- Relations between employees and employers are quite likely to be less tense when unemployment is high or rising. Employees will not want demands for a big pay rise to increase the chances of the business going bust.

- The very best time to recruit employees with scarce skills is when unemployment is rising. People with skills who have been made redundant will be looking for work. Usually, finding a skilled person means offering them higher pay than they are getting elsewhere. When unemployment is high or rising, this won't be necessary.

How might Nissan gain from the closure of the BAe Systems factory?

- When unemployment is rising, the economy is going into recession and for many businesses, demand for the product is likely to be at best stagnating and at worst, falling fast. Low levels of confidence in the future are like a wet blanket, making it very difficult for businesses to expand. Government incentives to take on employees, like the one on page 72 can help somewhat.

The IMF

Show your understanding

The International Monetary Fund (IMF) watches over the world economy and lends to countries that are having difficulty paying their debts. It does an annual health-check on each of its member countries.

When it came to the UK in 2011, it said "In the event of a prolonged period of weak growth and high unemployment, the Bank of England should try to stimulate the economy and the government should also consider temporary tax cuts." When the Fund came back in 2012 the situation had barely changed. The head of the IMF, Christine Lagarde, said "Policies to bolster demand, before low growth becomes entrenched, are needed." She suggested that the Bank of England and the Treasury should help the banks to lend more to businesses. She concluded that if existing measures fail to stimulate the economy, then the Chancellor should consider cutting taxes, or increasing spending, or both – i.e. Plan B.

List and explain all the ways in which each of these policies might help small businesses.

Chapter 13

Financing the costs of production

Herbs of Distinction

Rachel Highcroft set up Herbs of Distinction after being made redundant from her job in advertising. She had always been a keen gardener and chef and she spotted a gap in the market for mail order fresh herbs which customers could keep in their kitchen so that they would always have fresh herbs available.

Rachel already had a small greenhouse in her garden and some tools so initially she just had to buy pots, soil and seeds. She also paid to attend a one day course on setting up in business. Rachel planted her first batch of seeds and waited for them to grow. In the meantime she was busy building a website for her business and ringing lots of restaurants to try to create demand for her herbs. She paid for adverts in some well-known cookery magazines which she hoped would encourage potential customers to visit her website. After three months Rachel's first batch was ready to pack and send. Rachel was delighted at the packaging she had helped to design with a local box supplier: it was a bit more expensive than she had planned but she knew that it was important for the plants to arrive in a perfect condition. The revenue from this first batch meant that Rachel could afford to buy more pots, soil and seeds to start again.

Discussion points

(a) What different costs did the business face?

(b) Try to classify the costs: sort them into different groups. What categories did you use to classify the costs?

(c) Do you think all businesses face similar costs? Which particular types of business might face higher or lower costs than others?

Put very simply, businesses operate by taking *inputs*, changing them in ways that *add value*, and producing *outputs*.

Costs of production

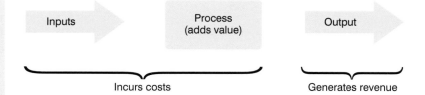

Outputs are sold in order to generate sales revenue. Revenue is money gained by the business when selling goods or services. The process of producing outputs incurs costs for the business. These costs of production must be paid for by the business. We can classify costs, placing them in different groups.

Classifying costs – starting up

Start-up costs

These are costs faced when an entrepreneur sets up a business. They are costs that only need to be paid once. They include:

- payments for services such as business advice and market research
- fixtures and fittings
- the tools, machines and specialist equipment that are needed to create the product.

These costs are usually paid before the business starts trading, so the entrepreneur will need to have sufficient finance to cover the costs until enough revenue is earned to pay them off.

Capital spending

In the case study above, Rachel's start-up costs included her initial stock, her training course and the packaging design.

Businesses can also incur significant one-off costs when making large changes or additions to operations. For example, when expanding into new premises or introducing a new product line, they may require new machinery or tools or staff training.

If Rachel's business continues to grow she will need a larger greenhouse and more equipment to use in it. This would mean a large financial outlay for Rachel which she would need to pay for somehow.

Investment

Start-up and capital costs include many items that would be classified as **investment**. When a business buys premises and equipment that will last for some time and make it possible to produce over a period of years, they are investing now in order to have sales revenue and profit in the future. Often, we regard spending on training or research into possible new products as investment too. Training makes employees more efficient and productive.

Start-up costs are incurred in setting up a business organisation.

Capital spending occurs when a business invests in fixed assets or something of long term benefit to the business.

Investment involves spending now which generates income in the future. It may involve buying capital equipment or spending on research or training.

Classifying costs – running costs

These are costs which an entrepreneur has to pay regularly while the business is operating. Literally, they keep the business running. Running costs fall into two categories: fixed costs and variable costs. Total costs include both fixed and variable costs.

Fixed costs

Fixed costs are not directly affected by how much the business produces. For example, insurance, utility bills and rent or mortgage payments have to be paid each month regardless of how much has been produced. These costs are not 'fixed' forever in terms of how much the business pays – it is likely that insurance costs will rise after the business makes a claim, for example. It is common for rents and utility charges to increase with inflation. The key issue here is that the level of fixed costs is **not linked to the level of output**. A rising level of output will not immediately affect the fixed costs of a business.

If a business grows significantly it is likely that fixed costs will increase, especially in the long term. This is because growth may require larger premises –this is likely to mean higher rent, utility and insurance costs. Additional staff may be recruited, increasing the overall cost of salaries. However, one extra unit of output will not directly incur extra costs in any of these areas.

Variable costs

Variable costs are directly linked to the level of output of a business. They are the costs of resources used to produce units of output, or to deliver a service. They include raw materials and the cost of labour used in the production process. If the level of output rises, total variable costs will also increase proportionately.

Labour costs can be fixed or variable. If a member of staff is paid a fixed salary regardless of how much work they do, they are incurring a fixed cost because it doesn't change according to output. If they are paid directly according to how much they produce (for example, piece-rate workers in a factory, or taxi drivers who receive a percentage of the revenue from each journey driven) then the wage is a variable cost because it goes up directly when the employee produces more.

Rachel's fixed costs at present are low – she just has to pay for the heat, lighting and water for her greenhouse and for any additional marketing she carries out. Her variable costs are everything directly linked to growing, packing and sending the herbs – soil, pots, seeds, packaging and postage.

Example

In Chapter 2 you met Tamara Knight, a massage therapist. When Tamara set up her business she had to pay a number of start-up costs. She had to buy a massage table, towels, uniform, first aid kit and a bag for transporting her equipment. She also paid for her qualification in massage therapy and a first aid course.

Now that Tamara is running her business she has to pay some monthly costs: she has public liability insurance, membership of a professional association for therapists and car licence and insurance costs for her car. These are all fixed costs because they have to be paid whether Tamara sees one client or a hundred clients. In fact, if she gave no massages at all, she would still have to pay these fixed costs.

Each time Tamara gives a massage she incurs some additional costs. She has to pay for petrol to drive to the client; she uses up massage oil and she has to pay to launder the towels and sheets used during the treatment. These are variable costs because the more clients Tamara sees, the more she will have to pay for petrol, oils and laundry.

Running costs are paid by a business organisation on a regular basis. Running costs may be fixed or variable costs.

Fixed costs are not directly linked to the level of output of the business. They do not change when output increases or decreases. These are sometimes called *indirect costs* or *overheads*. Fixed costs include all capital spending but also some regular costs such as staff salaries.

Variable costs are directly linked to the level of output of the business. They change as output increases or decreases. These are sometimes called *direct costs*. They include the cost of paying employees who are paid solely according to their contribution to the actual production process (direct labour).

Show your understanding

Think of a small business in your area. Make a list of the different costs that this business faces. Group these costs into start-up, and running (fixed and variable) costs. Identify potential capital spending that might be necessary as the business grows.

Now compare your ideas with your peers. You should see that different types of business will incur costs to different degrees. Some have high fixed costs and few variable costs (for example, hairdressing salons) and others have low fixed costs with much higher variable costs (for example, a mobile painter and decorator).

Chapter 14

Sources of finance

Abundant Ltd.

In Chapter 1 you met Shane Wall, owner of Abundant Ltd., and learned a little about his business history. In this chapter you will learn more about how Shane has financed his businesses.

When Shane first became a partner in Abundant Holidays he put in £12,000 of his own money. This was money saved from Shane's wedding disco business. This money paid the start-up and running costs of the holiday business and meant that hotels and DJs could be booked before all guests had paid in full for their holidays.

On taking full ownership of Abundant Ltd., Shane put in some more of his personal savings to get the business started. Initially he was not earning much from commissions so this money paid Shane a 'salary' so that he could afford his personal expenses. Married and with growing children by this time, Shane gave 50% of the company to his wife in recognition of the fact that their shared savings were funding the business.

Abundant staff raising their profile at an industry event hosting many potential customers.

In 2011 when the business moved to a larger office and took on new staff, Shane realised that he needed finance to cover the capital costs of expansion. With too little cash in the bank, Shane had to choose between approaching his bank for a loan and accepting an offer from a business associate who wanted to buy 25% of the business for £100,000. Shane turned down the offer and instead took out a large loan, committing himself for 5 years to high monthly repayments. The bank demanded that Shane provide his house as security for the loan – if the loan couldn't be repaid, Shane and his family would have to sell up, use some of the money to repay the bank and move somewhere smaller. Securing the loan decreases the risk for the bank but increases it for the entrepreneur.

Discussion points

(a) For what different reasons did Shane need finance?

(b) How might Shane have funded his business at each of the stages outlined above?

(c) Why do you think that Shane turned down the offer of £100,000 for 25% of his business and instead put his family home at risk?

You have learned already that businesses need finance for different reasons – to get the business started; to fund capital expenditure and to keep the business running. You might be wondering where this finance can come from. Broadly, finance can come from two sources: *internal* (from within a business) or *external* (from outside the business).

Internal sources of finance

Internal finance

Retained profit: once a business is operational it should be generating revenue. So long as total costs are lower than total revenue, there will be some profit. This profit can either be taken out of the business by the owner(s) as a reward for their enterprise, or can be retained and reinvested in the business. Retained profit can therefore be used to pay the costs of a business if necessary.

Remember that entrepreneurs usually (although not always) have profit as at least one of their motives. Retained profit cannot be paid out to the owner. The owner will have to be confident that the retained profit is being used to generate future value, or they are likely to prefer to take it as income for themselves.

Sale of assets: an asset is something of value. In a business this could refer to physical resources such as vans, machines, buildings, land or stocks, or it could be something less tangible such as a successful brand or a patent for a particular technical design. Any asset can be sold to generate cash which can then be used to cover the costs of a business.

Working capital: this refers to cash that a business has immediate access to. This is a simple source of finance for businesses with a good cash balance. Holding stock reduces working capital as the stock is paid for using cash and is then held by the business until it is processed or sold. A business needing to increase working capital can do this by reducing the total quantity of stock held.

> **Internal finance** comes from within the business. It can be *retained profit* or cash raised from the *sale of assets*.
>
> **Retained profit** is profit that can be reinvested in the business rather than being given to the owner(s) of the business in the form of income (unincorporated business) or dividend payments (incorporated business). It does not incur interest payments or dilute ownership of the business. It is a long term source of finance.
>
> The **sale of assets** can refer to physical assets such as machinery or property, or to intangible assets such as the patent to a particular product. It is a long term source of finance.
>
> **Working capital** is cash held by the business and used to keep day-to-day business going in the short run.

External sources of finance

External finance comes from individuals or organisations which are not part of the business. This finance is often in the form of *loans*, which have to be paid back, or it may be offered in exchange for **equity**. (Equity finance means that the business gets money in exchange for ownership of a **share** of the business.) This money does not have to be paid back. Sometimes it is possible for an entrepreneur to get a *grant*, which is finance that neither has to be paid back nor involves giving up ownership of any of the business. The government and certain charities such as the Prince's Trust offer grants to some businesses when they start up. It can also be possible to get low-interest loans from these organisations if entrepreneurs meet certain criteria.

Loans are one of the most common forms of external finance. The business borrows a fixed sum of money for a fixed period of time, making fixed regular repayments. The lender will demand interest as their reward for lending the money. Entrepreneurs may seek loans from a bank, or from willing family or friends.

The rate of interest will depend on a number of factors including:

- the current Bank of England interest rate
- the size of the loan
- the repayment period
- how the lender perceives the risk of the business defaulting on the loan (not paying it back).

Interest

Overdrafts are loans offered for short-term finance by banks. An overdraft allows a business to spend more money than is available in the business bank account. Effectively, an overdraft is an allowed negative bank balance. Interest is calculated daily on the overdrawn balance, usually at a rate higher than is charged for a fixed loan.

External finance

	For	**Against**
Loans	High Street banks may see well-established businesses as low-risk and give low-interest loans.	The higher the perceived risk, the higher the interest rate. New businesses may find it hard to get a loan from a bank at a low rate.
	For business start-ups, family or friends of the business owner(s) may provide finance, which is helpful if banks are unwilling to lend to an entrepreneur with no security and no trading history.	Often loans are secured on specific assets. If the business is unable to repay the loan, the asset becomes the property of the lender. The lender can sell the asset in order to recover their money. The most commonly secured assets are buildings which are used for long term loans. This is what happened when Abundant took out a bank loan.
Overdrafts	Overdrafts can be used to borrow a flexible amount for a short time.	A bank is able to cancel an overdraft at any time and request full repayment.
	As soon as money is deposited in a business bank account, it goes towards paying off or reducing the overdraft balance.	The interest rate on an overdraft is variable so changes in the Bank of England interest rate can be passed on quickly. This increases the risk for the entrepreneur.

Debentures are like long term loans in that they carry a fixed interest rate. The interest must be paid before dividends – so if profits are poor, debenture holders have priority over shareholders. But they are different from loans in that they can be sold in the same way as shares. (For this reason they are more often referred to in the press as bonds, or corporate bonds or loan stocks.) Debentures are a safe way for people and organisations to invest in medium-sized or large businesses, but because their interest rates are fixed, debenture holders do not benefit from extra profits when the business is doing well.

Venture capital is a form of long-term equity finance where an investor provides a sum of money for the business in exchange for a share of its ownership. Entrepreneurs generally seek venture capital when they are unable to raise the money needed through other channels, since giving up ownership of the business is long-term and reduces control over the business. It also means that any future profits will have to be shared with the venture capitalist. Venture capitalists are willing to take greater risks with their money than other lenders so are often used when, for example, banks refuse to lend to a business. Venture capital is usually sought where large, long-term investments are needed, for example to fund a business start-up or in the development and launch of a new technological product where there are high costs of design, development and production. Venture capitalists may offer advice and support to entrepreneurs as well as their financial investment. Some demand a say in how a business is run if they are to invest their money.

Example

The television programme Dragons' Den is based around venture capital. The Dragons are all venture capitalists who decide whether they are willing to risk investing their money in new business ideas. On the programme you can see negotiations between the Dragons and entrepreneurs where they decide how much money will be invested in exchange for a specific share of ownership of the business. The Dragons only invest in a business where they believe that their investment will generate returns, either from future profits or because the share can later be sold for more than the value of the original investment. In the case study, Shane turned down an offer like this.

Ordinary share capital is capital (money) raised by selling shares in the business. This can raise the large sums of money that may be necessary, e.g. to invest in the development of a new product or to fund the expansion of a business. Only incorporated businesses can raise share capital. (You will learn what this means in Chapter 15.)

Share capital

	For	Against
Share capital	Share capital does not have to be paid back and does not incur interest.	The original owner of the business gives up some control over it.
	Share capital can raise large sums of money for a business.	The new shareholder(s) will expect to receive a portion of future profits (dividends) as a reward for investing, so the original owner will receive less profit in the future.

Leasing is used by businesses that need land, buildings or equipment which they are unable or unwilling to buy outright. It is the name given to 'renting' an asset. Many businesses lease vehicles, or office equipment such as photocopiers, or office space. Leasing allows the business to avoid making one large payment – instead monthly payments are made to the owner of the asset.

	For	Against
Leasing	It is usually possible to upgrade the item leased, e.g. by switching a photocopier for a newer model on its release.	The business never takes ownership of the item.
	Maintenance and technical support are often included in the lease agreement.	The business will pay more than the market value of the leased items in the long term.
	Leasing is a more flexible way to acquire an asset than outright purchase.	
	Leasing can be used for long-term or short-term finance.	

Trade credit

Trade credit is short-term finance offered to a business by suppliers. It means that a business can receive goods or services from the supplier and pay for them later. For many businesses this means that there is time to generate revenue from sales to customers before costs have to be paid. Trade credit is typically offered for between 30 and 60 days although there is no limit to what a supplier can choose to offer, and it may be possible for a business to bargain for a longer credit period with some suppliers. In times of financial difficulty a supplier may shorten the credit period or limit the total credit offered because they themselves are short of cash.

External finance

Example

A bakery needs supplies of flour, butter and sugar in order to produce cakes for sale. The bakery bank account has a balance of £0 so there is no money available to pay for the supplies immediately. The bank has refused an overdraft on the account. Luckily, the supplier of these raw materials allows 30 days trade credit. This means that the bakery can receive the raw materials without having to pay for them and has time to bake and sell cakes, receiving revenue from these sales. By the end of the 30 day credit period the business has enough revenue in the bank account to be able to pay the bill from the supplier.

A **loan** is a fixed amount of money borrowed for a fixed period at a fixed interest rate. The loan is paid back in regular instalments until the total amount plus interest is repaid. Loans are medium- to long-term sources of finance.

An **overdraft** is a short-term flexible loan where a bank allows a business to operate with a negative bank balance. Interest is paid on the amount overdrawn, usually at a higher rate than is charged for a fixed sum loan.

Debentures (sometimes called bonds) are loans that can be bought and sold in the same way as shares. They have a fixed interest rate. They do not give part-ownership of the company but they are much less risky than shares, for the investor.

Venture capital is money invested in a new business by one or more individuals who believe that the business will succeed and therefore increase in value, but are willing to accept the risk that the business idea may fail. Venture capitalists may offer advice and technical support as well as finance. Venture capital is long-term and provided in exchange for a share of the equity of a business.

Ordinary share capital is long-term finance raised by selling shares in a business. Money raised does not have to be repaid. Investors receive part-ownership of the business and a share of the profits in the form of dividends.

Equities – another name for shares.

Leasing allows a business to use an asset without owning it, by making regular payments to the owner of the asset. Over time the total sum paid for the lease may be more than the cost of buying the asset outright. It reduces the need for external finance from other sources.

Trade credit is a short-term source of finance offered when suppliers allow a time period before payment for supplies must be made. The credit period will vary between suppliers and may be changed by the supplier at any time.

Find out

Visit the websites of two or three high street banks and compare the rates offered for small business loans. Calculate the repayments on a loan of £5,000 taken out over 5 years.

Find out the typical rate at the same banks for overdraft borrowing. Try to explain the difference between the two rates of interest.

Now research typical interest rates for these loans over the last 20 years. Discuss with your teacher how the current rate of interest for business loans compares to this, and how this might affect the decision by an entrepreneur as to whether or not to take out a loan.

Choosing a source of finance

The choice of finance in any situation will depend on three main factors:
- what the finance is needed for
- the resources of the business
- the objectives of the business owner(s).

Short- or long-term?

The first consideration is the purpose of the finance. How much is needed and for how long? The principle of *matching* says that the source of finance chosen should suit the purpose. So a long-term financial commitment, such as buying a new office building, would require a long-term source of finance. A short-term purpose, such as paying for stock, should be funded through a short-term source of finance, perhaps working capital or overdraft facilities.

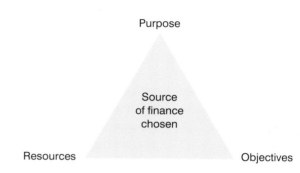

The resources of a business will partly determine the sources of finance available. 'Resources' here is used in the same way as in the acronym LOSER. (This is explained on page 2, in the Introductory chapter.) Clearly, retained profit is only available to a profitable business and share capital is not an option for a sole trader. Loans will be easier to find if the business has a successful trading record or assets to offer as security.

Internal or external?

The objectives of the owner(s) will also influence choices made. Some entrepreneurs would prefer to retain full control of their business so take out loans rather than give up equity in their business. Others are uncomfortable with the notion of being in debt or don't want the stress of meeting repayment deadlines. In this case equity finance may be a better choice than borrowing. Entrepreneurs who have growth as an important objective may not be willing to wait until they have enough retained profit to fund expansion, preferring to raise external finance in order to achieve their objective more quickly.

Entrepreneurs must consider different sources of finance depending on their own objectives.

WATCH OUT!

Whilst retained profit is often the preferred source of finance for a business, it is too simplistic simply to state that 'this business should use retained profit to fund xyz venture'. Remember that all choices incur a *trade-off* of some kind. The use of retained profit assumes, of course, that the business has sufficient profit available to it, but it also means that the owner(s) of the business cannot benefit personally by receiving the profit in the form of dividends. If this does not suit the *objectives* of the owners at the time, retained profit will be an inappropriate source of finance.

Exam style question

Carol and Richard Faulkner have a love of food and of cooking. For many years they have talked about opening up their own restaurant and now they are finally doing it. They have taken out a 12-month lease on a site in their local town centre, furnished it in a simple, homely style and chosen a menu that is getting very positive feedback from customers so far.

Both Carol and Richard gave up well-paid jobs in order to start the restaurant and, although they are currently living on the last of their savings, neither regrets their decision. They are enjoying the excitement of running a new business and the freedom which comes from being their own boss. They are hoping that the restaurant will break even in the next 6 months and be profitable by the end of the year.

1. Briefly explain two sources of finance that Carol and Richard could have used to fund the rental and furnishing of their new restaurant. *(8 marks)*

2. Carol and Richard chose to fund their business idea using a bank loan as well as personal savings rather than to borrow money from friends and family. Evaluate the merits of their choice. *(9 marks)*

Chapter 15

Business structure

Legal
structures

Tamara Knight and Abundant Ltd.

By now you are familiar with Tamara and Shane and some of the key features of their businesses.

Tamara's business is small. She buys little stock and runs her business from the summer house in her garden. Her spending is low and she never owes more than £100 on her business credit card. If her massage work ended tomorrow, Tamara would not earn any more money, but nor would she be in debt. Tamara is a sole trader. You will learn about sole traders in this chapter.

Shane, on the other hand, runs a much more substantial company. The business has commitments to large, regular payments. There is the rent on the office in central London and salaries for 15 employees and freelancers, not to mention the repayments on the loan he has taken out. If Abundant stopped getting work now, Shane would be responsible for significant ongoing costs. It is unlikely that there would be sufficient cash in the bank to pay all of these costs so the assets of the business may have to be sold to raise more cash. Even this may not be enough. With creditors knocking at the door, Shane wants to be sure that his personal possessions won't be taken to pay any outstanding debts. Abundant is a private limited company. You will learn more about this type of ownership in this chapter.

Discussion points

(a) What concerns might an entrepreneur have when setting up a business, specifically related to their personal assets?

(b) What actions could an entrepreneur take to protect his or her personal assets from business debts?

Any entrepreneur setting up a business has to choose the legal structure of that business. Broadly, the two choices are either *unincorporated* or *incorporated*.

Unincorporated businesses

An unincorporated business is one which is legally indistinguishable from the owner(s). A **sole trader** has one owner and a **partnership** has more than one owner. These are easy businesses to set up – the owner(s) simply has to inform HMRC that the business exists and to keep records of business income and expenses. At the end of each tax year the sole trader or the partners must complete a tax return and pay tax on their income. They must also pay National Insurance contributions. (HMRC stands for Her Majesty's Revenue and Customs.)

Sole traders

The advantages of setting up as a sole trader are that the entrepreneur has full control over the business and gets to keep all the profit. However, it can be hard to raise finance since the sole trader may have limited personal savings and banks may see the business idea as risky, reducing their willingness to lend to the sole trader.

Sole traders have *unlimited liability*. This means that they are legally the same entity as their business and are fully responsible (liable) for its actions. If the business incurs debts which it cannot pay, for example by buying stock which cannot be sold or letting utility or rent bills build up, the sole trader becomes personally liable for the business debts. This means that the sole trader's personal assets (cash, possessions, property) could be used to repay the business debts. This is a significant concern for sole traders who operate businesses with high running costs because the potential debts will be high.

Partnerships

Unincorporated businesses

A partnership can be beneficial because there are more owners to contribute finance (and to help run the business). However, profit must be shared and there is the potential for conflict in decision making. In addition to this, each partner is *jointly liable for all debts*. This means that each individual has unlimited liability for all of the debts, even if they were incurred because of the actions of a partner in the business. This means that partners must have complete trust in each other. Partnerships work well for solicitors and other professionals. They work less well for businesses that will face heavy capital spending from the start.

> A **sole trader** is an *unincorporated* business owned and operated by one person. The sole trader may employ workers but it is most common that they work alone. The sole trader has unlimited liability for the debts of his/her business.
>
> A simple **partnership** is an *unincorporated* business owned and operated by two or more individuals. The partners are *jointly and severally liable* for the debts of the business – this means that they are each individually responsible for all of the business debts.

Incorporated businesses

When a business is incorporated it gains its own separate legal identity. This means that debts incurred are the debts of the business, not the owner(s). So personal assets cannot be used to repay business debts. This is called *limited liability* – the liability (responsibility) of the owner(s) for any debts is limited to the money invested in the business by the individual. This means that they can potentially lose all their investments but their personal assets are not at risk.

Limited liability

The owners of an incorporated business are called *shareholders* since they own a share of the business. One person can be the sole shareholder of a business or shares can be sold to others in order to raise finance for the business (you read about this in Chapter 14). There are two types of incorporated business: private limited companies (with the suffix Ltd.) and public limited companies (with the suffix PLC).

Private limited companies

Entrepreneurs setting up in business would use a private limited company (Ltd.), selling shares only to people they know. In exchange for part ownership of the business the entrepreneur can raise significant finance to invest in the business. In return the shareholders will receive part of the business profit in the form of *dividends*. Some shareholders may want to have input into how the business is run while others will be happy to receive their dividend without having any regular contact with the business. There are more regulations governing private limited companies than sole traders and partnerships, which increases the cost and complexity of administration in running the business.

Sole traders	Private limited companies
Advantages	**Advantages**
Full control of the business	Limited liability for business debts
Owner receives all profit.	Easier to raise finance.
Disadvantages	**Disadvantages**
Unlimited liability for all debts	More regulation
Can be hard to raise finance.	Sharing the profits
	Shareholder involvement.

A partnership is an unincorporated business owned and operated by two or more individuals.

Public limited companies

PLCs

Public limited companies issue shares publicly and are governed by many more regulations than private limited companies. This is not an option for entrepreneurs when setting up a business since the initial share offering must raise at least £50,000. This is very unlikely for a business with no trading history! Public limited companies must publish their financial accounts each year – you can read the accounts of many well-known businesses by searching through their websites to find the pages where this information is published.

Find out

Use the website www.businesslink.gov.uk to find out more about the processes involved in setting up different types of business organisation.

Unlimited liability means that an individual has no legal separation from their business and is therefore personally responsible for the debts of the business. Their personal assets could be used to pay business debts if the business assets are not sufficient to pay debts incurred.

Limited liability protects shareholders of incorporated businesses. This means that the individual is not fully liable for the debts of the business, which is legally separate from the shareholders. The most that shareholders have to contribute towards business debts is the amount of capital originally invested in buying shares.

The owners of **private limited companies** have limited liability for business debts but cannot raise finance from the general public. They are often family businesses and the shareholders are members of the family or personal friends. They are usually small or medium-sized businesses.

Public limited companies (PLCs) are owned by their shareholders, who have limited liability. The companies can raise finance by selling shares to the general public and large organisations such as pension funds. In this way they can raise substantial finance in order to expand.

WATCH OUT!

When writing about sources of finance, remember that share capital is only an option for incorporated businesses. For small businesses this means that they would need to be a private limited company rather than a sole trader or partnership.

It is a good idea when considering issues related to business structure and finance to balance out benefits, such as the ability to raise share capital, with drawbacks such as increased administration or loss of some control and some of the profit.

Exam style question

Shanaz Begum had always loved fashion. At school she put on fashion shows and by the time she was at college she was funding her social life by making accessories for her friends. After completing a university course in fashion, Shanaz was ready to set up her own business making and selling bags and scarves.

With large personal debts built up as a student, Shanaz knew she would need to raise capital to fund her business start-up idea. She decided to create a private limited company, selling shares to a tutor from her college and also to two family members.

1. Briefly explain two factors that Shanaz would have considered when deciding on the legal structure of her business. *(8 marks)*

2. Assess the impact on Shanaz' future business operations of her decision to set up as a private limited company rather than as a sole trader. *(12 marks)*

Estimating sales levels, costs and profit

Clinton Cards

Founded in 1968, Clinton Cards grew to be the biggest card retailer in the UK. It employed over 8,000 people in 767 high street stores when, in May 2012, it went into administration. This was despite the greetings card market actually growing overall, partly because there are now more occasions than ever for which a celebratory card is available ('you are pregnant', 'you're getting divorced' and 'you passed your driving test' are just a few examples of these). Clinton Cards lost £3.7m in the 6 months to Jan 2012 and, with recent like-for-like sales revenue 3.5% lower than the previous year, struggled to generate enough income to cover all of their costs. Eventually their creditors called in debts which the business couldn't pay, forcing Clinton Cards into administration. Perhaps a competitor should produce a 'we're sorry to hear that your business is in trouble' card.

Discussion points

(a) Why might sales revenue have fallen in 2012? What could Clinton Cards have done to increase sales revenue during this time?

(b) Apart from falling revenue, for what other reason(s) may Clinton Cards have made a loss in the previous six months?

(c) Clinton Cards had been operating at a loss for some time. Why is it not possible for a business to survive when it is not making a profit?

You have already learned that businesses are set up in order to achieve specific *objectives* set by the owners, and that objectives can be *financial* or *non-financial* in nature. Even where the business is driven by strong non-financial objectives, such as ethical reasons or to contribute to the local community, profit is still important for the majority of entrepreneurs. This is because the entrepreneur is giving up their time and effort to run the business, and the profit made is the reward for their time and effort and the risks they are taking.

Profits and losses

You have learned that: **PROFIT = REVENUE – COST**

In the example above, Clinton Cards was making a *loss* rather than a *profit* because costs were higher than revenue. In this chapter we will explore the profit formula in more detail, investigating how entrepreneurs make decisions which affect their overall level of profit. By the end of this chapter you should be able to answer the questions on Clinton Cards in more detail, using precise business language. If you need to, revise the content of Chapter 13 on costs.

Revenue

Revenue is money coming into a business. *Sales revenue* (also sometimes called *turnover*) is earned through the sale of goods and services. A business may also receive revenue from interest payments, dividends or royalties paid by other businesses. Here we will concentrate on sales revenue.

SALES REVENUE = SALES VOLUME x SELLING PRICE

Or   **SR = SV x SP**

Where SV = the quantity of goods/services sold   SP = the price charged for each good/service

Therefore, in order to maximise sales revenue, an entrepreneur has to balance the total number of units sold with the revenue earned from each sale. As you learned in Chapter 5, for a normal good an increase in price will lead to a fall in demand. If buyers are very sensitive to a change in price, an entrepreneur may maximise SR by setting the SP lower than that of a competitor and hoping to increase the sales volume substantially.

> **Profit** is the money remaining from sales revenue after all costs have been paid. It is the entrepreneur's reward for investing their personal resources (time, enterprise, assets) in a business and taking risks.
>
> A business makes a **loss** when revenue earned is less than costs to be paid.
>
> **Revenue** is money earned by a business.
>
> **Sales revenue** is money earned by selling goods and services. It is calculated by multiplying the sales volume by the unit selling price.
>
> **Sales volume** refers to the number of goods or services sold by a business in a period of time.
>
> **Selling price** is the amount charged to a customer for the purchase of a good or service.

Identifying a pricing strategy to be used

The price charged must be profitable – that is, it must cover the *variable costs* of producing the product and also contribute towards the *fixed costs* or *overheads* of the business. An entrepreneur can use a range of strategies for setting prices:

Cost plus pricing

This is a simple method of setting prices. The entrepreneur calculates the costs of production and adds on a percentage of this as a *mark-up*. This represents the profit made on the sale. It is a simple calculation as it requires no additional information or market research – only cost data from within the business.

Deciding on a price

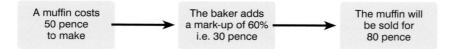

This approach suits entrepreneurs who want a very simple pricing strategy. It will also work well if competition is not based on price but focuses instead on sources of competitive advantage, such as quality or convenience. However, it does not take account of the price of competitor products or consider likely demand at this price.

Competitor based pricing

This strategy suits businesses in very competitive markets where sales are particularly sensitive to price. It involves the entrepreneur carrying out research into prices charged by competitors and then setting a price either in line with this or slightly below, in order to attract increased sales. This strategy requires some investment in market research in order to ensure that prices remain competitive over time.

Think

The well-known tag line of the John Lewis Partnership is 'never knowingly undersold'. Why might this be such a successful strategy for this particular business?

Premium pricing

Some products are differentiated by quality, targeting consumers with high incomes and aspirations. In this case the consumer may view a high price as an indication of the quality of the item, increasing its perceived value. The entrepreneur may choose to price the item at a premium (a particularly high price), in order to reinforce this perception.

This strategy is generally more successful with products targeted at *niche markets*, rather than at consumers in a *mass market*, where price competition tends to be more important to sales.

Price discrimination

This strategy involves charging different prices to consumers in different segments of the market, for the same product. Some of the most common examples are student discounts given in many high street shops, or cheaper off-peak fares charged on rail and bus services. This can be a good way to 'smooth' demand for services by encouraging customers who are flexible to use the service at a less busy time. A hairdresser may offer a discount to pensioners on Tuesday afternoons when there is little custom, encouraging the pensioners, who have more free time than other clients, to free up appointments at times when other customers may be competing to book an appointment. This strategy only works where groups are clearly identifiable and where it is not possible for the product bought at a discount to be re-sold by the customer at the higher, market price.

The importance of the correct pricing strategy

'Price' is one element of the marketing mix, the others being 'place', 'product' and 'promotion'. These four aspects of a product or service work together to create an offering which attracts customers. It isn't possible to say comprehensively that one is more important than another – if any element were inappropriate for a customer it would reduce the value perceived by that customer and reduce sales. It is correct, though, to say that the price charged should be in line with the other elements of the marketing mix. This is why Primark can successfully (and very profitably) sell low-priced (and low cost) clothing and accessories, while at the same time Louis Vuitton sells their branded clothing and accessories at a much higher, premium price, equally profitably.

> **Cost plus pricing** calculates the cost of producing a product then adds a percentage of this cost to arrive at a price. The added amount is called the *mark-up*.
>
> **Competitor based pricing** takes account of prices charged for similar products in the market, setting a price similar to or just below this.
>
> **Premium pricing** charges a high price for the product, above the market price. This reflects the high quality of the product itself and may help to convey matching customer perceptions of the quality.
>
> **Price discrimination** charges customers in different market segments different prices for the same product in order to reach as many customers as possible.
>
> The **marketing mix** is a model for considering different aspects of a product and its market. Also known as the 4 'P's, the aspects are price, place, product and promotion.

Sales volume

This refers to the quantity of the product sold over a period of time. Many entrepreneurs set a specific objective of increasing sales volume. At any given selling price, the higher the sales volume, the higher the total revenue.

Sales volume typically increases when prices are lowered. Other strategies which can be used to increase sales volume involve adapting different elements of the marketing mix. For example:

Pricing strategies

Using the marketing mix

Promotional activity

Advertising, sponsorship and effective public relations can all increase sales volume for a business. Promotion can encourage existing customers to purchase more or attract new customers to the brand. However, these activities incur costs so an entrepreneur should ensure that the forecast increase in sales volume will generate enough extra revenue to more than cover these costs.

Modify the product

Updating a product so that it meets customer needs more effectively can give the product competitive advantage and attract a greater number of competitors.

Alternatively, changing the way that customers *use* a product can lead to increased sales volume. Advertising for Kellogg's Special K breakfast cereal recently suggested that it could be used as part of a weight loss programme if eaten for breakfast and lunch, with a main meal in the evening. Straight away this doubled the amount eaten by individuals who were used to eating cereal only for breakfast and now ate a second bowl for lunch each day.

Increase availability of the product

Making a product available in new geographical areas (a different part of the UK, or exporting to new countries) or through new channels in existing markets (in stores as well as online, for example) can increase sales volume because more customers have easy access to the product.

Increasing profit

At the beginning of the chapter we used the formula:

$$\textbf{PROFIT = REVENUE - COST}$$

We can expand this formula using what you have learned about revenue and about costs. Remember that

$$\textbf{SALES REVENUE = SV x SP}$$

and, from Chapter 13, pages 78-79:

$$\textbf{TOTAL COST = FIXED COST + TOTAL VARIABLE COST} \text{ (the variable cost per item x SV)}$$

Still following this? In which case, we can say that

$$\textbf{PROFIT = (SV x SP) - (FC + (VC x SV))}$$

and this is a *very important* formula because it highlights all of the variables which affect the profit made by a business. To increase profit:

Making a profit

- a business can seek to increase sales volume
- or it may raise the selling price
- or it may look for a way to cut either fixed or variable costs.

The most successful strategy would be to aim to achieve all of these goals at the same time, since this would generate the largest increase in profit.

Show your understanding

Think of a small business in your area. Working with a partner and using the expanded formula for profit above, explain to each other all of the different ways that the business could act to increase its profit. Be as specific as you can, giving examples and suggestions related to the business. Discuss each part of the formula in turn.

Finally, decide between you which strategy you think would work best for your chosen business. Make sure that you can explain your reasoning clearly.

A muffin costs 50 pence to make ⟶ The baker adds a mark-up of 60% i.e. 30 pence ⟶ The muffin will be sold for 80 pence

Pricing strategies *(margin heading)*

Margins vary

Profit margins can be compared from year to year. A good profit margin would not be the same for all businesses. Supermarkets tend to have small profit margins, because every item has to be bought in and the supermarket simply sells it. It does not actually create the products. A manufacturer of electrical products would expect higher profit margins because much of the work done to create the product will happen in the factory.

A small business would concentrate on increasing its profit margins, year by year. Larger businesses can sometimes compare their profit margins with those of similar competing companies – if they can get access to the accounts.

Gross profit margin is gross profit as a percentage of sales revenue.

Net profit margin is net profit as a percentage of sales revenue. It can be used as a performance measure, giving a view of how successful the business has been, in comparison to past years.

Show your understanding

In fact, Daniel decided to pay himself the same in 2012 as he had in 2011. But he did raise his price from £38 to £41, + P&P. He felt that the quality of his work was such that he could still sell the same number of bowls at the higher price. His reputation as a craftsman was growing by word of mouth and he felt his market was growing too. He was right – sales volume stayed the same in spite of the price increase. Calculate both gross and net profit margins for 2011 and 2012.

Using profit and loss accounts

Budding entrepreneurs who need to attract bank finance or to impress individual investors must produce estimated P&L accounts. Established businesses need to look back at the accounts from the past for a whole range of reasons:

Analysis

- to identify trends over time. These can be very revealing.
- to raise finance, as proof of past performance. The bank will want to study all the accounts carefully.
- to analyse the success of the business in meeting its profit objectives.
- to compare with those of others in the same industry, in order to judge efficiency.
- to set objectives for the future.

Improving profits

Daniel could see from his profit and loss account in 2011 that he would need to do something. He was lucky in that getting better known was creating interest in his product: many new businesses fail in the first few years. But putting the price up worked for him. He could have considered many alternatives though: using cheaper wood, cutting the price and hoping to make and sell more, moving to cheaper premises and so on. In general, these are the possibilities:

- *Reducing COGS* can mean using the available labour more efficiently, or cutting the cost of inputs, perhaps by finding a cheaper supplier.

Decisions

- *Reducing overheads* can be achieved by doing administrative tasks more efficiently or finding cheaper premises or suppliers (e.g. for insurance). In extreme circumstances, pay may be reduced – as in the period 2008-12 (see Chapter 11, page 65.)

- Increasing sales revenue by *raising prices*, but only if the market is growing, as the price rise will not put people off. If in fact there is a cheaper competing substitute for the product, this will not work.

- *Cutting prices* can increase sales revenue if it means selling to a wider market. Some businesses can move from a small niche market to a mass market in this way. But the business would have to look carefully at the increase in COGS as a result of increasing output. There might also be an increase in overheads, such as marketing expenses. Trying out different possibilities using break-even analysis might help to analyse the likely outcomes.

Competition

Exam style question

Sharples Technology Ltd

Sarah Sharples decided to set up a business which could support and maintain small business IT systems. This involves identifying appropriate hardware and software for her clients, setting up their IT system and customising it to the individual needs of the business. She has been quite successful in recent years because she can combine IT expertise with excellent customer service. Sarah's profit and loss account is shown below.

Sharples Technology Ltd – Profit and loss account, year ending 31 December, 2011

	£	£
Turnover		450,000
Cost of sales	300,000	
Gross profit		_____
Overheads		
– Rent, rates and insurance	22,000	
– Heat and light	1,000	
– Administrative expenses (including pay)	80,000	
Net profit		_____

Then, 2012 saw a change of fortunes. A competing business set up nearby, a subsidiary of a much larger company. Sharples Technology lost some of its market share. Sales fell by 20%. Cost of goods sold fell proportionately, but overheads remained the same.

Questions

1. Calculate the missing figures for gross and net profit in the P&L account above. *(4 marks)*

2. Calculate the following for both 2011 and 2012.
   (a) Gross profit margin
   (b) Net profit margin *(8 marks)*

3. Using the figures you have calculated, explain what has happened to Sarah's profitability.
   (8 marks)

4. Recommend two strategies Sarah could use to increase her net profit margin. *(10 marks)*

Chapter 19

Creating a business plan

Rooms to rent

John and Tracy have lived in Margate, a fairly small seaside town on the Kent coast, for years. Margate has until recently suffered from a poor reputation and little investment. Now, however, the town is on the up and is returning to the tourist map. There is a new art gallery on the seafront which is helping to attract visitors, especially since an upgraded train service means that they can travel from London in a little over an hour. The local council is also investing money in renovating an historic entertainment venue and investors are buying up cheap local properties.

John and Tracy have a large house on a street by the sea. Their grown-up children have left home and Tracy is considering converting the house into a bed and breakfast business, renting out rooms to tourists and business visitors. Neighbours on local streets have already set up their own businesses, which charge between £40 and £90 a night per room. Tracy is confident that they can make enough money each month so that she can give up her job in the town's tourist office, to be available to look after their guests.

Discussion points

(a) What start-up and running costs is the bed and breakfast likely to incur?

(b) What questions should John and Tracy ask themselves before committing to setting up their new business?

(c) Adapting their family home to become a bed and breakfast will cost the couple money, which they will need to borrow from their bank. How might they persuade the bank manager to lend the money they need?

If you've ever watched the television show Dragons' Den, you'll be familiar with the sight of nervous entrepreneurs struggling to respond to the relentless questioning of the 'dragons' – a panel of venture capitalists who decide whether or not to **invest** their money in the business ideas pitched to them. Members of the panel typically fire questions at each entrepreneur. These focus on different aspects of the business idea, such as the details of the product or service; projected sales and revenue figures; market data and targets for growing the business. Each 'dragon' must be satisfied that any money they invest will be used to generate future profits, or they will choose not to invest at all.

Making a plan

Whilst the Dragons' Den is a television format, the questions asked of the candidates on it are typical of the questions that any entrepreneur should ask themselves when developing a new business idea. Any new business incurs *opportunity costs* – the entrepreneur gives up time, usually money too, resources which could otherwise be invested elsewhere. So the business idea needs to be worth the risk taken with these resources. The construction of a **business plan** is a common way to explore the business idea and to reduce the risk that it will fail.

Investment means spending now that will yield income in the future. It can mean investing in one's own business, either to start up or to expand, or taking a part share in someone else's.

Business plan – a written document detailing all aspects of a business idea. A business plan includes information on the product or service, marketing, production, human resources, equipment needed and financial information.

> **Business planning** – the process of carrying out market research and thinking through a business idea in order to construct a business plan.

What is a business plan?

A business plan is a written document which contains detailed information on different aspects of a business idea. It is a formal report used by the entrepreneur for their own planning and also to support applications for finance for the business idea. A business plan completed with care and diligence is likely to take some time to construct because of the need to carry out market research and to prepare financial information.

The purpose of business planning

In the case study above, John and Tracy need to ask themselves many questions.
- Can they afford the initial conversion work to their house?
- How much demand will they be likely to have now and in the future?
- How might demand vary over the year – few tourists visit the seaside in winter?
- How much profit can they hope to make?
- How much competition will they face?

The issue of competition is important: they need to identify a secure source of competitive advantage. Writing a business plan will help John and Tracy to address these questions in a thorough and logical way.

Competitive advantage

Completing a business plan helps to reduce the risk of the business idea failing, since potential pitfalls should be identified early and can be addressed. It forces the entrepreneur to consider many different aspects of their business idea:
- how it is different from competing products
- who it is aimed at – the target market
- how it will be marketed
- the costs of production.

Most entrepreneurs will need some sort of financing either when starting their business or, later, when seeking to expand. A key purpose of business planning is to provide evidence to support the gaining of finance. This could be from investors or from lenders. As in the Dragons' Den example above, investors or lenders will want to make sure that their money will be used effectively and that it will generate a return.

By reading the business plan they can make an informed decision about whether or not to invest – a solid business plan significantly increases the chance of gaining funding.

A third purpose of business planning is to give focus and direction to a business. The plan should identify targets for the business over time, such as plans for expansion or profit targets. Clear goals can help to motivate entrepreneurs as well as provide a measure against which to compare progress over time.

The fourth purpose, supporting monitoring and evaluation, is important because the circumstances surrounding the business can change unexpectedly. Will everything go according to plan? Probably not. As changes occur, the situation can be compared with the scenario set out in the business plan. This will help in devising ways to adapt to change.

The flow chart shows the process. There may be good reasons why targets are not met, but action may be required when things do not turn out as expected.

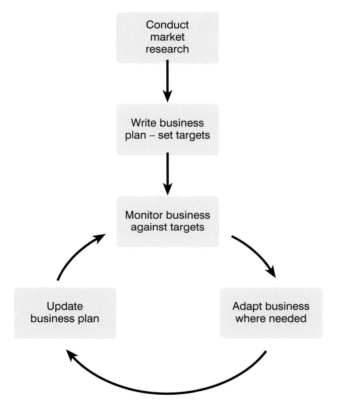

Constructing a business plan

Market research

Templates for writing a business plan can be found easily online or in business start-up packs provided by high street banks. These give suggested structures which encourage an entrepreneur to consider all aspects of their business. In order to answer many of these questions, entrepreneurs need to conduct research – they are likely to use many of the methods of primary and secondary market research which you learned about in Chapter 8. Although this can be time-consuming, the more detailed the research which supports a business plan, the more useful the plan is likely to be in helping the entrepreneur to achieve their objectives.

> **Find out**
> The website www.startups.co.uk contains lots of information for entrepreneurs considering starting their own business. Use this site to find out more about business planning – what it is, why it is useful and tips for successful business planning.

A business plan contains detailed information on different aspects of a business idea.

The features of a business plan

There is no one format which must be followed in writing a business plan. Whatever approach is taken, the following information will typically be included:

- *Product or service to be produced* – detailed drawings, descriptions and images are needed to show what the business will produce and sell.

- *Marketing plan* – shows how the business will be marketed including the pricing strategy, how and where it will be sold and advertising or promotional activities to be undertaken.

- *Production plan* – saying how the product will be produced or the service delivered. This should be detailed, identifying sources of added value and of competitive advantage.

Information required

- *Premises and equipment needed* – this is a list of all capital items as well as consumables used in producing and delivering the product or service.

- *Human resources plan* – an outline of staff needed including numbers, working hours and training necessary. Personal details of staff are not necessary, although it is common to identify the specific skills and experience that key staff will need, where these will contribute to the success of the business.

- *Sources of finance* – how the costs of the business will be financed, at start-up and once the business is in operation.

- *Profit and loss forecast* – providing a prediction of the profits or loss generated by the business in the first few years of operation. (It may be clear from the start that the business will take time to become profitable.) This should be based on detailed research and should include the different measures of profit which you learned about in Chapter 18. It is good practice to compare predicted profit margins to typical margins for businesses in the chosen industry.

- *Cash flow forecast* – this is a summary of how cash is predicted to flow into and out of the business. It is important because without adequate cash to cover costs, the business may not survive, even though it could be profitable in the long run.

Cash flow forecasting

Cash flow

As you have learned, businesses incur costs and generate revenue. A key issue for many businesses is that payments, or *outflows*, may be needed before revenue, or *inflows*, are generated. In the case study at the beginning of this chapter, you can imagine that John and Tracy would have to spend money on washing towels and bed linen and on buying items for breakfast before guests arrive, but would not be paid until guests leave. In this case, the outflows may only occur a day or two before the inflows and are relatively small. But imagine how different this might be for a builder installing a new conservatory, or for a pharmaceutical company developing a new medicine.

A cash flow forecast aims to predict when cash outflows and inflows will occur. This enables the entrepreneur to identify times when finance will be needed to cover any cash shortfalls – they can then seek a source of finance appropriate to the amount of money and the length of time for which it is needed. One of the main causes of businesses failing, or becoming **insolvent**, is poor cash flow management, rather than a business idea that is basically unprofitable. For this reason, an entrepreneur needs to be sure that they have sufficient working capital to bridge the gap between spending on costs and receiving revenue.

Cash flow forecast – a month by month prediction of the timing of expected cash inflows and outflows in a business.

Cash inflows – money coming into a business. This includes revenue, investment and borrowing.

Cash outflows – money leaving a business. This includes fixed and variable costs as well as cash withdrawals by the business owner(s).

Insolvency – when a business fails because a sustained lack of working capital means that debts cannot be paid.

⚠ WATCH OUT!

A business can be basically profitable but, because of poor cash flow management, can fail. Make sure you are clear on the difference between *working capital* and *profit*. (Working capital was covered in Chapter 14, page 81.)

The limitations of business planning

A business plan isn't a guarantee of success, but the process of writing the plan should help to identify key issues which can be addressed if necessary. Obviously, the more skilled an entrepreneur is in carrying out and interpreting market research, the more accurate, and therefore useful, their plan is likely to be.

Making the plan work

You have learned that a business plan can give focus and direction to a business. This will only happen if the entrepreneur makes time to return to their plan regularly, reflecting on progress and making changes to the business where necessary. A business plan does nothing on its own, sitting at the back of a filing cabinet. It cannot make up for mistakes like failing to keep in close touch with suppliers or to communicate effectively with employees.

Finally, a business plan needs to be updated regularly to reflect changes in the market and the business. The best business plans are flexible working documents – up to date information gives the people running the business a better basis for decision making and therefore increases the chance of the business succeeding.

Sources of help

The BIS website (created by the Department for Business, Innovation and Skills) has much useful information. Local business advisers are often also able to provide advice to individual businesses. The Prince's Trust provides some funding for unemployed or disadvantaged people under the age of 30 to start their own business. Producing a business plan sometimes reveals that the potential entrepreneur is not yet ready to strike out on their own in business – which can lead to a good decision not to go ahead yet. Taking time to get more advice can be a good move.

Exam style question

1. Explain why a bank might want to see an entrepreneur's business plan before deciding whether to offer them a start-up loan. *(6 marks)*

2. Briefly outline the content and purpose of business planning for an entrepreneur. *(6 marks)*

Index

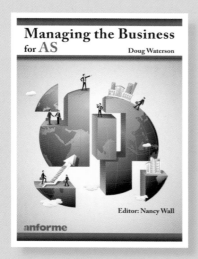

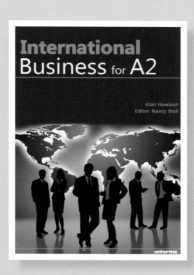
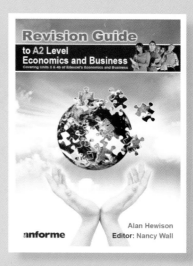

Anforme Limited

Stocksfield Hall

Stocksfield

Northumberland

NE43 7TN

Telephone: (01661) 844000

Fax: (01661) 844111

email: info@anforme.co.uk

Visit our Website at www.anforme.com